Becoming UnFamous

The Journey From How We Do It To How *He* Do It

Montell Jordan

www.montellandkristin.com

Ryan Sprenger, Print Broker. Printopya.com
Interior design by Renee Evans | reneeevansdesign.com

ISBN: 978-1-942306-61-0
Printed in the United States of America

DEDICATION

I would like to thank my wife and greatest love of my life, Kristin Jordan. My children Christopher, Catharine, Sydney, Skyler & Samantha; you are all the realization of promises kept. To my Mom & Dad, brothers and sisters and my entire family, I honor you. Nana, thank you for your strong arms that picked Alabama cotton and still hugged me just yesterday. Thanks to everyone responsible for both my music career successes and failures, as they all contributed to the man I am today. Thank you to anyone who has said prayers for me to succeed and for those who have unsuccessfully prayed for my downfall. Thank you, church families from my childhood until now, for rightly dividing the word of truth and allowing me a place where I get to be at peace being one person, the Montell Jordan God loves the most. Thanks, Dennis & Colleen Rouse, for your spiritual parenting of kids who dream really big. Thank you, Craig Obrist Photography, for your making me beautiful with your photography and Stephanie Pendleton for your creativity and artwork for this project. Thanks, Mallory Cruz, for your editing and journeying alongside us in both our real and literary lives. Thanks, Rick Warren and Saddleback Church, for your support and influence. Thank you to the additional proofreaders, editors, printers, and distributors of this book. Lastly, but really firstly, thank you, Father, Son and Holy Spirit, for the incredible things you promised you would do in the lives of those reading this book. Thank you, God, for more than a hit song and a good story; thanks for breathing life back into me to breathe into others.

CONTENTS

The New Montell

I laid at the altar tonight, Wednesday, August 25th, 2010.

I have left my tears, a multitude of them, at the feet of Jesus.

I am uncertain of what is to come, what life will look like following this submission, or how to even move forward after this act of faith but it is finished. Fame has been crucified.

I have heard the message of Christ's crucifixion so many times before, but tonight was different.

I have decided to completely entrust God with my life, direction, career, provision, ministry, and everything else.

I have conceded that I am weak and incapable of doing His Will. He will have to use me. I cannot do this on my own. Without Him I will fail. If "I can do all things through Christ Jesus who strengthens me" is real, now is the time that I charge Him to prove it.

I am certain I will look like a failure to some, a has-been to many, and a hypocrite to most; I only hope to look like my Savior to ONE.

I can't go back, and there's no purpose in going

forward if He isn't coming with me. My flesh man is terrified of the unknown, yet my Spirit man is unafraid and optimistic...

At 41 years old, the second half of my life begins tonight. I will write and tell the story of what God does.

As I type into my phone, now sitting in the second chair, center aisle to the right, four rows back, I have limited words. It is difficult to look into the faces of those around me tonight because I don't feel the same. It is obvious that I'm not who I was just hours earlier. I am changed.

Without even speaking to my wife (who I have caught occasional glimpses of sprawled on the church floor while picking myself up), I am certain we are with one accord in regard to the drastic turn of events that are about to occur. Once again, there's no need to even begin this journey if God is not gonna get the glory from this.

My son Skyler, 6, is holding me now. He can feel something is different, but I'm certain he doesn't know what it is...and neither do I.

God, here I am. I'm not sure exactly where that is, but as long as You're with me, here am I.

INTRODUCTION

fa·mous -1. *Having a widespread reputation, usually of a favorable nature* 2. *Renowned; Celebrated* 3. *Known to be recognized by many people.*[1]

You don't have to be famous to become unfamous.

It is my desire that, while sharing my life experience in a digestible, understandable, relevant, relatable and useful format, anyone reading these words, those rooted in faith and those searching for answers, would gain some form of direction for their life from mine.

Allow me to begin by saying that once upon a time I was famous; now, I am a dead man walking. I realize that's a pretty interesting way to begin a book, but hang in there, and I will explain.

Self-preservation is one of the most universal behaviors in humans. Most everything living will fight to survive. But what happens when that instinct needs to be violated? What is the process that needs to occur in order for a human to have a desire for himself or herself to die? And why in the world would anyone in his or her right mind want to go against this survival characteristic anyway? I did this, and throughout this book, I will share why and how.

On January 2nd of 2011 I left the R&B recording business and went into full-time ministry. While I believe this process has allowed me to exchange success for significance, many don't understand that someone had to be assassinated in order for this new life to begin. I had to die; I also had to order the hit.

Now please don't get me wrong, I'm not speaking to you about a physical murder or suicide; I'm speaking about the death of our flesh and our fleshly desires in exchange for the life of the spirit man and woman that lives inside each and every one of us. I am more alive today than I have ever been, absent of fame, notoriety, riches, and the cares of the world. If you knew me in my previous life and then saw me now, there would be no question in your mind that I am truly back from the dead.

Funny enough, the day I began writing this book was a non-unfamous day. That particular morning I was recognized by 3 people while simply trying to put a quart of oil into my car.

I was dressed moderately and simply and I didn't have myself groomed in anyway that would've drawn attention to myself. Naturally, being 6'8" tall there is an inclination for people to notice my *Goliath-like* features when I pass by, and afterwards they will either give the "I know him from somewhere, but I don't wanna stare" look, or "Is that Montell Williams?" or "Is that "Michael Jordan?" or the several different combinations of recognizing someone but not being able to put the name with the face. Once I'm gone and far enough away they finally realize "oh gosh, that was Montell Jordan." It's also quite possible that while people are trying to figure out if I am famous or not, they hear the faint song "This Is How We Do It" playing in the background of their subconscious. Fame is often accompanied by a musical soundtrack. I found it interesting that the same day I would begin sharing my experiences about the journey to becoming unfamous, it was as if God was showing me what happens when He fulfills the promise that "I will make your name great."

During the last five years I have been on a journey that I'm finally realizing I've been on for the last 46 years—or my entire life—without knowing the destination. Until now. Statistically, this means I have spent less than 3% of my entire life completely dedicated to what I was ordained, designed, called, and created to do. And I've been in church most of my life. The reality is that even in church, I was functioning in my gift and not in my *calling*. We will explore this once we actually get into my life.

I was commonly asked, "Montell, what's it like to be famous? Doesn't it bother you that you can't even walk into a room without everyone noticing?" I would reply, "It would only bother me if I walked into a room and no one noticed." I will later share that there was a harvest to be reaped from that mentality that did not result in a healthy garden.

The purpose for this book is to present to you, both famous and folks who desire to be famous, the template, the blueprint, the road map—perhaps even the treasure map—that I personally used to guide me to where I now function happily and completely in what I was created and destined to do. My story just may trail blaze a pathway in a direction that you may have been seeking without even knowing it. For anyone who has ever desired to become famous, I know the secret. I also know the cost.

I'm not sure this journey is for everyone, but I'm hoping that exposing the details of my journey from R&B

music, unfaithfulness, alcoholism, you name it, into a full life in Christ will assist anyone else who will take the same leap of faith and walk the same pathway that I did. Unlike me, you will have some type of direction sign to help you navigate the journey.

There will be stop signs, yield signs, danger signs, warning signs, "what the heck are you doing" signs, detour signs, flashing lights, U-turns, you name it. This journey for you is going to be full of them, just as it was for me. But take heart and be encouraged, as the signs I will be sharing with you will hopefully help lead you to the correct destination.

In closing, allow me to take all the guesswork out of where this story will end. The destination is Jesus Christ. With that being said, that ultimately is everyone's goal, whether they are aware of it or not. I've often heard that a wise person learns from the mistakes of others while a fool learns from his own. So for those who want to know how we do it, how He empowers and enables us to die to ourselves so that we may not only have life more abundantly and eternally but also live more fulfilled here in the now, This is How HE Do It.

Choose wisdom. Share my life.

PASTOR MONTELL JORDAN

ONE

What's in a Name?

I was born Montell Du'Sean Barnett on Tuesday, December 3rd, 1968, around 2:32 a.m. at John Wesley Hospital, just 4 days before my mom's 18th birthday. I have always shared a special connection with my mother, probably greatly due to the fact that she and I existed before my adopted father or younger brother and sisters came along. At birth, my last name was *fatherless*.

I have always known that I was different. For as long as I can remember, my mother has told me I was "special." (And she didn't mean it in the *little yellow school bus* sense of the word either!) Even when I was a baby, she said she saw I had a mark of ministry on my head. My name was *special*, she would tell me. And because she was my mother, I believed her.

As an infant, I was given the nickname "Monkey" because of my small round head, tiny ears, and predisposition to being carried on someone's hip over walking. Although this was only my family nickname, later throughout my R&B music career I would secretly keep the nickname as I sometimes felt like the caged zoo animal that people often watched from a distance, sometimes speaking within earshot and pointing

13

as though I could not hear or understand that they identified me as someone "famous." It can be awkward and intimidating meeting someone famous, so I always tried to extend grace when someone finally mustered up the courage to walk up to me, point, smile, and sing "This Is How We Do It" as though it were my name and that they weren't doing something that had been done a million times before.

I wasn't born into a famous family. Quite frankly, I was an original product of "baby mama drama" long before the term was even entered into urban slang. I have never met my biological father, Edward Fitzgerald Barnett, and have only seen one or two photos of him. It is my understanding that although he attempted to take responsibility for me as a child, him not wanting to commit to marrying my mom was the deal breaker that not only kept he and I from relationship but also cemented my adoptive name change from Barnett to Jordan upon my mom's union with my dad, Elijah Jordan, a few years later.

So my story begins a little something like this: single-parent teen pregnancy produces a black, fatherless baby boy, born into the ghetto of South Central Los Angeles, California.

I was raised up in the Baptist church (or the *black* church in my case), which would become my very first musical training ground. Every weekend was like a family reunion as most of my relatives were all members of the same church and served in some area of ministry. My pastor during this time was one of the most influential men in both my musical and spiritual life. Unfortunately, sometimes those we admire and respect are often most capable of doing the most damage. Pastor

Richard Stubbs is now in heaven, and I honor him and his memory. I recall an instance as a preteen, possibly 11 or 12 years old, where he said something to me that took many years to recover from. One day *The Rev* pulled me aside and asked me a few questions.

"Do you know why your family has to struggle so much sometimes?" he asked.

I replied, "No."

He then asked, "Would you like to know why?"

I answered, "Yes, sir."

"It's because your family's last name is *Jordan*." He continued. "In the Bible, the Jordan was considered to be one of the filthiest rivers known to man. It was dirty. *Bad luck.* Your father has that last name and he has passed it on to you. Do you know what that means?"

I answered, "No, sir."

"It means that you will always struggle. So long as you have the last name Jordan, you will always have a mark on you because it is *unclean*. Nothing will ever come easy for you or your family."

According to the pastor, my name was *dirty.* My name was *bad luck.* My name was *struggle.* My name was *unclean.* My love for him allowed me to accept his definition of my name.

After hearing these words spoken over me, I felt I would always have a strike against me. I was just an impressionable kid, and at this time in my life, I still didn't know that I had been adopted (I wouldn't find this out until I was 16 years old.) My family (like many) had a way of keeping secrets (family business), and I'm certain I'm not the first person to realize that sometimes really good Christians do some really bad things. All my family members and the church folks around me knew my birth circumstances, yet they were protecting me until I was old enough to handle it.

I would learn the hard way about the power words have. Life and death are in the power of the tongue, and the man I identified as being the closest person to God was instructing me as to the trials that would lie ahead for me because of my *name*. He spoke those words into my life and into my spirit. Because I loved and respected the man with everything that was in me, I received those words as truth. The Jordan name was my inheritance, however this encounter devalued it.

Even in the presence of an earthly father, the unspoken words over me were resounding: fatherless, unwanted, undesired, unworthy, and unclean. Sometimes it is what goes unsaid that speaks loudest. So what's in a name? *Everything.* This way of thinking would result in years of destructive behavior, misguided ideals, insecurities, and self-esteem issues.

On a good note, there was a musical impartation that The Rev left in me that I will always be grateful for. He was a great man, and amidst those words came the development of my musical gift. Thankfully, God would erase the negative words from my life and propel me into my destiny, yet this inner healing wouldn't occur until well into adulthood. Until then, I began to use adversity as fuel to move forward into my future. Sure, the Jordan River may have been filthy, but it was also the place where Jesus directed the leper to dip himself seven times, and there, he was *healed.*

TWO

The Gift of Music

Growing up I felt like my parents were the black MacGyvers, because although we lived check to check, they somehow managed to make something out of nothing. We considered ourselves to be a middle-class family and church and family were often synonymous. Church was everything for me: my afterschool programs, my summer vacation, and ultimately, my musical training ground. I would hear all the time, "Montell, you're going to be a preacher one day." I would think to myself, "You must be *out of your mind*. God didn't tell *me* that." Back then, I never knew God used people, situations, and circumstances to communicate to His people, much less to me. Keeping it real, I didn't know or care what He had to say. Still, I heard it over and over again my entire life from people both inside and outside of the church.

This is important to know because like many of you reading this, I was called into ministry at a very young age yet I did not answer. I knew that beyond talents and gifts, I was anointed for something great, but I didn't comprehend why I was given the musical and influential leadership that I had. Who in their right mind would want to be in ministry when they could be famous? I appreciated The Rev and his position in the church, but really, reverend over rock star? Pastor over NBA player? Minister over millionaire? No way! Honestly, I didn't know a kid in my neighborhood who didn't want to be famous, liked, popular, respected, admired, rich, and talented. We all understood some of us were more talented than others, but none of us could comprehend what it meant to be anointed.

A gift is something given to us all. Gifts come from God, and once He gives them to us, He does not take them back. These gifts are activated through talent or anointing. Talent is something you work at to do well, while anointing is something you don't work at, and God works through you. Essentially, talent shows what *you* can do with your gift, while anointing shows what *God* can do with your gift.

Anointing isn't just something that the church has cornered the market on. In many different professions, we need certain abilities to achieve higher levels of success. On the job, in sports, even in our own personal desires outside of the church, God gives gifts to people who sometimes excel, just not always for His glory. Athletes, businessmen, musicians, speakers, and teachers can all carry an anointing in their profession. Anointing enables someone ordinary to do something extraordinary.

For several years, The Rev would take me and a few other talented and gifted young teenaged kids to a little church on the corner of 51st and Hoover, seat us on the front pew, and then proceed to wrap a 3ft. chain around the door, locking us inside. I look back now with spiritual eyes on the symbolism present during that season and understand that he wasn't trying to keep us from being disturbed or to stop anyone from getting in.

He was preventing the impartation of the anointing into us from getting out. We would play musical instruments for a minimum of 6 hours daily, nonstop.

Talents can be taken away, gifts cannot. They come without repentance and cannot be revoked, even from the Lord Himself. Anointing is transferrable. This was made evident in the biblical teaching where a double portion was transferred to Elisha upon receiving the mantle from Elijah. The Rev was passing on the musical anointing (mantle) on his life to those he recognized with the gift.

God gives us all gifts. The challenge is not only to identify what our gifts are but also to know what they are for.

As kids we all wanted to become famous. It didn't matter if we would become famous singers, wrestlers or athletes; we just wanted to be a famous *somebody*. My personal driving forces toward this direction included a desire to escape the inner-city poverty mentality, the negative name association spoken over my life, and the achievement of one day rescuing my mom and family from the hood so I can look into the camera and perform the ever coveted "Hi, Mom" wave to show that a young black man had done well.

So the transfer began. We would become some of the best child musicians and singers in all of Los Angeles during the late '70s to early '80s. Our foundation was rooted in the more traditional styles of music from James Cleveland, to Andre Crouch and The Hawkins family, yet admittedly, our fresh take on gospel derived more from pop music culture and the movement that was happening outside of the church. In the black church, long before the terms "praise and worship" were defined, the songs were simply summed up as "and now we will have an A & B selection from the choir." And although we loved groups like *Commissioned* and *The Clark Sisters*, MTV, R&B, Pop, and Hip Hop began to run through our veins, and we took every opportunity to introduce what we learned from the secular world into the sanctuary, knowing the older generation was clueless to every James Brown rhythm, Michael Jackson baseline, and Prince turnaround we played. Quite honestly, we had no idea that we church kids and gospel musicians would one day become some of the forerunners to evolve the style of '90s R&B music and be the catalyst prompting these musical worlds to collide.

We would form music groups (the first group I ever sang in was called the Christian Stars of Life) and eventually travel throughout LA as though we were on a mini-tour of local Baptist churches, participating in their recitals and Sunday evening programs.

One of my most vivid memories I can recall was making a pact with one of the most influential kid leaders of all our youth, Shappell "Shep" Crawford. He was my God brother, and our families were extremely close. He was Magic Johnson, and I was "the Cap" Kareem Abdul Jabbar of the Lakers. One day we made an arrangement.

"If either one of us ever gets famous, we will make sure to come back for the other." We even went as far as to say, "and when you become a Pastor, I will come and be a Deacon at your church." I would be the first to get the opportunity to make good on our agreement.

We were introduced to the gift of music, appointed and anointed for ministry. I enjoyed playing and singing music for God, and those were some of the best times of my childhood. But somewhere deep down inside,

I knew I was destined to be famous. The athletes we admired were famous. The singers we mimicked were famous. The wrestlers we imitated were famous. We were popular within our immediate circle, and for a couple of neighborhood kids, that little bit of influence could go a long way. I didn't know how far it would take us, but I personally was ready for the journey.

THREE

Gifted vs. Called

I've often been asked, "Do you play basketball?" which was always immediately followed by, "Man, if I had your height, I would be in the NBA." It's almost as though people think being tall is a guaranteed ticket to stardom, absent of preparation, skill, luck and opportunity. Unfortunately (or maybe fortunately), I was neither gifted in this area nor have I ever believed I was called to be an athlete. The truth is, I was more musical than athletic in my childhood, and although I attempted to advance in athletics later in life, showing up to my high school at 6'3" with the last name Jordan lacking the ability to dribble or dunk a basketball compared to the kids who dribbled out of the womb thwarted those dreams pretty quickly.

Being a church pianist as a child would lead to many facets of advancements in musicianship. I was a pianist, vocalist, saxophonist, arranger, songwriter, composer and director, exercising these gifts mostly within the church. I recall sitting at an old used piano in our living room, looking out of the front window and watching my brother and our neighborhood friends laughing, running and playing games. I was inside, being forced by my dad to rehearse. The Jacksons had Joe, Venus and Serena had their dad, and I had mine.

The way I practiced and the way The Rev imparted music into me didn't train me to read music but, instead, I was taught to "play by ear." This was mostly to accompany his preaching and to be able to follow him as he prepared to "whoop" on Sunday mornings. I didn't realize it at the time, but this would hinder my ability to read music later in life, as I wondered, "Why learn to read when I can mimic and imitate what I hear?" I have never been proud of this limitation, but God would enhance my gift of playing by ear in other creative areas of music, so that although I couldn't read and play music that already existed without hearing it, I could play music that *didn't* exist.

I would hear melodies and harmonies all the time and from the age of 12 into my mid twenties, I could not sleep without having music on. I believe the Lord was trying to speak to me in His "still small voice" even back then, but the sound of music drowned out His. I can only imagine what I missed: the dreams He wanted to share, the direction He wanted to show, the confirmation He wanted to give, and the fellowship and intimacy He wanted to have with me. He knew me and wanted for me to know Him, yet I was simply too busy appreciating the gift more than the gift-giver.

It becomes dangerous when we exalt gifts over God, not only outside the church but also inside the church. Without the proper perspective on what our gifts are for, we can find ourselves loving singing *about* God more than actually loving God. We can love to preach and teach *about* serving God more than actually loving to serve God. Ultimately, we may find ourselves functioning in what He has gifted us to do yet not what we are *called* to do.

This is where I constantly found myself. From the church choir stand to my high school senior talent show singing Lionel Richie's "Jesus Is Love" to the DJ equipment in my college dorm room to the Budweiser Best in the West talent showcase to talent shows at USC and Cal State Northridge to Monday nights performing in Pasadena at the Crystal Penny Showcase in front of Shanice Wilson and Janet Jackson to singing and dancing with my college friends Chicago and Ant Money in our R&B group "2X Da Swing" in the living room of a Motown Records A&R (who upon hearing us advised we go into gangsta rap) to being turned down by label owner Barry Hankerson because although he liked me he had already signed a guy named R. Kelly, I began to function in what I was gifted to do, not in what God called me to do.

I was still sort of an entertainment chameleon during this season, as I would take on the identities of many of my musical influences. I had no idea what Montell Jordan was supposed to sound like. I could imitate Luther Vandross, Stevie Wonder, Michael Jackson, and Prince, and my sense of humor even enabled me to imitate Eddie Murphy imitating Luther Vandross (taken from his famous Kentucky Fried Chicken stand-up routine— but the extra-saved people reading this book won't get that at all). As New Jack Swing came upon the music scene, and I was emulating *Aaron Hall* from the group Guy and memorizing his ad libs, vocal inflections, and runs, I still somehow could feel a spiritual connection to God, even though the topics sung in R&B were far from holy. I could feel God when I listened to Stevie Wonder, and to date, Innervisions is still my favorite album of all time.

How was this possible? It wouldn't be until many years later upon entering into full-time ministry that the Lord would entrust me with His revelation on the Power of Music and answer that question for me. I assure you, it was possible. I actually felt closest to God when I was either playing or listening to music, no matter what genre. Whatever spirit the music was purposed for when created was what would begin to manifest in me. So if a dance or party record like Marvin Gaye's "Got To Give It Up" played, I would dance. I loved music, and the songs I would listen to began to attach themselves to my soul and influence me to respond according to what the spirit behind the music prompted.

My musical experiences would gradually evolve into a mild form of compulsion. As I advanced (or regressed) from ministry-directed worship into consumer-driven performance, I would find myself seeking to be the center of attention and adoration, whether I was singing gospel songs or not. In church, I looked to hear how well I did and how I took the church into the spirit the way I sang that song. In the nightclubs, I was often told how it was crazy that I didn't have a record deal yet while women were bringing money up to the stage and laying it at my feet.

This was the gift God gave me. I was musically directing and leading people to the destination of my choosing. I was in church my entire childhood. I "did" church. The reality was, although I was in church, in many ways the church was not in me. I could direct them toward God, yet I couldn't lead them to Him. You can't lead someone where you haven't been. I was a worship leader long before I ever knew I was leading worship. Sadly, not all worship leaders are in church. True, I was given a gift from God but I did not know how to use it responsibly. I was preparing to take this God-given ability and use it to glorify myself over Him. The crazy thing is that God knew what I was about to do, and He allowed it to happen. My future life in ministry was about to be learned not in seminary, but in the music industry, and every trial and test that I would experience would later become our testimony. I say "our" because I was not entering the music business or the next phase of my life alone.

FOUR

Let's Make a Deal

In my full-length autobiography, I detail how I got my first record deal. I have found that those who believe they have nothing are often the ones willing to risk everything. Many upcoming and developing artists don't know the difference between flexibility and compromise. This reality is not only prevalent today or even 20 years ago when I first entered the business, but possibly since the beginning of the music business itself. To my knowledge, one can be flexible and not compromise who they are. However, in my experience, I didn't even know who I was, so I was willing to make compromises believing I was being flexible. Elijah Jordan is an amazing dad, yet I didn't have the confirmation of a biological father, and ministry spoke the words of eternal struggle over me. I imitated every artist I listened to and loved. I was seeking a sound I could be identified with because I didn't know what Montell Jordan sounded like. I would often say I loved music so much that I would do it for free; I didn't realize music was listening to me when I was offering my life service *gratis*. The mindset of most struggling artists is to do whatever you've got to do to get in. Once you're in the door and you sell some records and experience some success, you may seek to gain some leverage. I had nothing, so in my mind, I had nothing to lose. Some people think by entering the business to be successful you are required to sell your soul to the devil. This is false. Like me, some can freely give pieces away at no cost.

In 1993 I produced a demo funded by John Singleton, a friend, fraternity brother, and movie producer. He had great interest (but not much time) in getting involved in the music business. He brought on Paul Stewart, known in the business as "DJ P," as his A&R executive. DJ P was my liaison between Singleton's venture, New Deal Records, and myself. Because John was still focused on his filmmaking career, he and I rarely interacted. Meanwhile, DJ P and Singleton parted ways and Paul made alliances with Russell Simmons, president of Def Jam Records. It wasn't long before I was asked to go with DJ P's Power Move Productions (PMP) and sign a recording contract. I avoided the advances of PMP for several months, but after becoming frustrated with delays and failed communication efforts with New Deal, I desired to be "put on" so badly I eventually abandoned the loyalty of my fraternity brother and went along with Paul.

I traveled to New York City and spent an entire day with industry mogul Russell Simmons. Throughout the day I met hip hop musical icons like LL Cool J and Run (before he was a Reverend); Russell spent most of the day ignoring me, talking on a cell phone call that seemed to last at least 12 hours. The evening ended in the parking entrance to Tens, a strip club in Manhattan, where I would perform a cappella in the backseat of Andre Harrell's Range Rover. When I was done, Andre gave Russell the approval that I was worth signing to a deal. Andre was the president of Uptown Records (Mary J Blige, Jodeci), and his confirmation of my musical ability prompted Russell's response for me to "go home and get a lawyer."

In my original deal, I committed to record a Hip Hop/ R&B album for $130,000. The finances and terms of the agreement were non-negotiable. The deal was structured for 7 albums or 10 years, whichever came first. Once I had signed the short form of the contract, $40,000, the first of 3 installments would be delivered, and I would begin working on my first project until the long form of the contract was completed. The documents were finally ready, and on December 31st, 1993, I signed with PMP Records. I didn't know at the time but the offer from the parent label (Def Jam) was for nearly $350K, and the production company (PMP) basically received the other $220K. I don't blame DJ P, my lawyer at the time, or anyone else for that matter. You just don't know what you don't know. I was being taken advantage of while celebrating the fact that I had just secured a recording contract!

All that to say, here is some perspective. My first recording contract was horrible. *But* it was a deal, meaning it was what I agreed to. Deals are made daily throughout the industry where companies are offering you a small percentage of a new life inside of the music business or you can keep 100% of the life you currently have outside of the music business. Some of the worst music business horror stories surround musical talent who were willing to give up almost everything for very little, as opposed to keeping 100% of nothing. I don't know what the going rate is on integrity these days, but it happens in nearly every industry: *people are willing to accept less than they are worth.* I am not discouraging anyone from entering into contracts or agreements; I am encouraging everyone to understand what they are actually agreeing to. *It's called a deal for a reason.* Here is a sobering truth: five #1 singles and nearly 10 million albums sold worldwide generated more than $100 million in sales for my label. Twenty years later, I still receive royalty statements documenting I am still un-recouped by several million dollars. This means I am still indebted to the label, or that I still owe and will quite possibly always owe the company money. You do the math.

I traveled back to California having the assurance of a recording contract with one of the most reputable and street credible brands in the business. I felt good. I went on to be one of the first R&B recording artists ever signed to Def Jam records and became a musical predecessor to what became the Def Soul imprint. At the time, I was simply known as "Russell's rap-singer." Russell pitched me as having the ability to document street life in south central LA the way a rapper lyrically would but with the delivery of a solid vocalist. I was singing what West Coast rappers like NWA were rapping about. It was this R&B meets Hip Hop presentation that would eventually become my signature calling card, my very own unique style that would begin to develop and distinguish me from R. Kelly and the other male artists competing for that R&B space during that season. I would write rap lyrics and then add melody to sing the words over beats and tracks. There may have been a few other artists attempting this as well but, really, I did it best. And even if that wasn't the case, for some reason I believed I was chosen to do something great—just as I was told from birth—and it was beginning. *This was the formula that I used to create what didn't already exist.* Instead of getting on the bandwagon, I became the bandwagon that, a year later, everyone would be riding *while tipping up their cups and throwing their hands up.*

This musical journey officially began when I was 18, and by age 25, I had officially secured a deal. It had taken seven years, but to everyone else, I was an overnight success. What people didn't see was the culmination of years, months, weeks, days, hours, minutes, and seconds that happened leading up to the evening I fell asleep and woke up a success. At least now everyone knows that overnight success does not actually happen overnight.

FIVE

Love Under New Management

Kristin Jordan is now the love of my life, yet there was a time I did not know Kristin Shai Hudson existed. Throughout my pre-Kristin dating experience, I was in two good church-girl relationships, a reckless loss of my virginity at age 19 early in a college relationship, which lead to multiple sex-without-commitment relationships and ultimately landed me in a relationship where I thought I had found the right girl, knowing I was the wrong guy. This may seem like normal behavior to anyone outside of the knowledge of faith. After all, living together, sleeping together, and having sex outside of marriage, in efforts to satisfy ourselves is pretty commonplace these days. I mean, isn't it a good idea to "test the waters" and see if this is the right person for us? No, no it's not. Inside of faith, this is known as *sin*. Fornication, or sex outside of marriage and living together (or "shacking up" as the old church folks would say it) were my methods of operation into my first few years of college. I was living in sin. If you are reading and hearing this for the first time, this simply means I was living to satisfy my own fleshly desires outside of the way God designed and desired for me to experience real love, passion, sex, and relationship within the covenant of marriage. I was, in essence, seeking to experience all these things He created, but outside of the safety of marriage where He created it to be experienced. Although it may feel good to our physical body, our spirit never gets satisfied so the flesh seeks to answer this void by repeating the action again and again, thinking it will quench the thirst and fill the emptiness. But it cannot. Manmade solutions cannot fill a space that only God was meant to fill. Perhaps you are also living in sin and the life and actions I described above may define the life you are living now. Here is where I present the truth to you in love. What I have explained as being sin may probably cause some to feel condemned. Those who feel *condemned* probably have no desire to change their behavior, see nothing wrong with living for today, and their hope is outside of faith. They have that choice. For others, what I have explained as being sin may cause you to feel *convicted*. Those who feel this conviction feel the tug on their heart from God, probably not knowing it is God reaching out to them, and you do have a desire to change your behavior. Even if you don't know how, the good news is there is hope. You also get to choose. That hope is inside faith, and as I continue to share my journey, perhaps you may experience the joy in the hope I have found in faith. Through all my sinful exploits, I had finally come to a place where I was tired of manufacturing counterfeit love and passing it off to others as real. I desired the one He had for me.

Kristin and I had been around each other for years prior to us actually ever meeting. My cousins knew her, and our fraternity and sorority brothers and sisters all ran in similar circles, but our paths had somehow never crossed. It was as though she was hidden, and I would have to find her. I believe God wouldn't allow me to see what He had for me until I was prepared to accept and choose His plan over my own. I had to get to a place where I desired what He wanted for me more than what I wanted for me.

When we did eventually meet, it was love at first sight for me; it was love at second sight for her. Admittedly, Kristin didn't actually see me during our first meeting. We danced a bit, talked a little, and she laughed her way through a night where she didn't really want to be with a new guy she really didn't care to know. Once again, this was confirmation that I found her. Following our second meeting (which was our first actual date), she saw me for the first time in all my splendor! I did get a second chance to make a first impression. From that double date, we would become inseparable.

From that time in the fall of 1991 we would both begin to experience major transitions. She would be given an ultimatum to choose her sorority allegiance over our relationship. Most women in her position would have never chosen a man over an organization that took a year to join, both physically and mentally. I would watch my longtime friends become more distant and even angered as I positioned Kristin to hold the most valuable place in my heart. Most men in my position would never have chosen a woman over a friendship, yet this was more than romance over bromance; there was something about our connection that went beyond physical intimacy, compatibility, and feelings of love. Somehow, even though she wasn't brought up in church, we both knew the Lord was drawing us together. There is a difference in feeling and knowing. Kristin was the one God designed for me, and even though I had found the right one, we would go right back to our default form of relationship over the next few years and experience living in sin, or outside of God's covenant, in exchange for immediate gratification. We lived together, were intimate together, and did life together. We experienced all the privileges of marriage without the promises.

We both loved music and decided we could build a career in it together. Kristin Hudson was sharp, strong, sexy, and independent. Her managerial style was intimidating to some, but in my mind, I wanted someone I could trust. To my dislike, she would advise me to leave my college music group and the groups we were producing and pursue a solo career. I would do this, and to my surprise, many opportunities began to present themselves that were not previously there. This was difficult for many who were around us at the time.

I sometimes reflect on how Jesus had 12 disciples, yet sometimes He would only take Peter, James, and John with Him. Even though He had 12, everyone wasn't designed to go where He was going or to see what He was going to experience. I was no Jesus, of course, but as I later strived to become more like Him, I would understand this concept more and more.

During this season just prior to securing the record deal, I had gone through many different management scenarios. Kristin had my heart early on in this music business journey and eventually became my manager. When our personal relationship experienced some turbulence, I became uncertain of a girlfriend/manager scenario. At one point, she had female partners who worked alongside of her. In an attempt to balance the managerial power, I added my fraternity brother and my aunt (as a spiritual advisor) to the mix. I literally had a five-person management team, one of the largest and most confusing in Def Jam history, according to them. Over time, this team would eventually evolve (or dissolve) into just Kristin and my trusted Kappa Alpha Psi fraternity brother, Tom Cunningham.

There was a lot I didn't know about the music business, and I knew far less about love and relationships. The one thing I did know was how to follow my heart. My mind and flesh had given me all the reasons to stay single while entering the music industry, but something deeper inside me, inside my spirit, told me that I would need Kristin to be able to survive the journey to come. We had gone through a series of makeup to breakup situations during our 2 years of dating, yet we both felt certain that the Lord placed us together. There was this unwritten and unspoken rule that if you were not married prior to entering the music business, there's no way a relationship can survive. I had gotten a record deal and both our careers were about to take off, so I knew what I had to do.

I knelt down on one knee and asked Kristin to marry me at a French restaurant called the *Moustache Café* that was located on Melrose Blvd. in Los Angeles on Valentines Day in 1994. I sang an original song to her in the center of the restaurant. The ring was placed in a champagne glass that our maître d' nearly had to force her to take (because she didn't drink) and our chariot was a white limousine that would drive us out to Malibu beach while Jodeci's "Feenin'" played on the radio. We celebrated by calling our family and friends to announce our engagement.

SIX

Married to the Music

Immediately following an engagement, I understood it was customary to set a date for a wedding ceremony. I never expected in exactly four months and four days from the time I proposed we would be saying, "I do." We agreed there was no need for a long engagement considering the album release was scheduled for August, and we knew I would be leaving to go on tour if things went well.

I began working on the album with a producer named Oji Pierce (who is now deceased), while Kristin worked on the wedding plans. I presented Oji with the idea that I had been working on for *Slick Rick's* "Children's Story," and together he helped me enhance the track even more. I was still learning my way around my equipment, and he was extremely instrumental in helping me purchase the correct pieces and teaching me how to use them. The task was now to try and top the song "Somethin' 4 Da Honeys," one of our first recordings that we knew everyone was feeling.

During the wedding planning phase, I would learn a valuable *man lesson* from this process. "Whatever you think is best, honey" is NOT an acceptable response when it comes to planning the day most women have envisioned since childhood. Whenever she asked me about my thoughts regarding the flower arrangements, invitations, catering, or anything, I had to at least form an opinion. Men, take my word for it: if you are not part of the solution, you become part of the problem. Save yourself the grief and be prepared to formulate and express your opinion (only when asked!), even over the smallest things. The big day was scheduled for Sunday, June 18th, 1994. It was Father's Day.

It is worth noting that many months prior to our engagement and wedding planning, Kristin and I experienced a major breakup. During this time, we completely separated. It was also in this season apart that she found the Lord and her life was transformed. Early on during our dating, I introduced her to the church, but she didn't really have a relationship with Jesus until our separation. She soon realized that we had been living in sin, which she was oblivious to before. She prayed for the Lord to remove me completely from the picture if I was not the one He had chosen for her life. The more she attempted to "pray me away," the more I was unknowingly drawn closer to her. When she finally agreed to allow me back into her life, it was at specific times: 11 a.m. on Sunday mornings and 7 p.m. on Wednesday evenings, both during regularly scheduled service hours at her church. Twenty-something years later, we believe this separation needed to occur so the Scripture that says "what God joined together, let no man separate" could be realized. In order for us to truly be inseparable, He would have to be the one joining us together. During this period, although neither Kristin nor I could ever regain our virginity, God restored our purity.

The big day finally arrived and all our family and friends had gathered together at the Joy House, an outdoor garden located in Inglewood, California. We had a few hiccups. My groomsmen fraternity brothers got drunk prior to the ceremony, and I had an (unexpected) almost hand-breaking "welcome to the family" from my fiancé's uncle. The keyboardist somehow forgot the power cord to provide the music, so I did what I had to do. I prepared to sing the soundtrack to our wedding day.

As I stood at the front altar of our outdoor church and looked down the aisle, I saw an angel. Her wedding gown was amazing. She looked flawless. She had been secluded so as to not have any worries regarding the already delegated responsibilities for the ceremony. All she had to do on that day was prepare herself to be married. Oblivious to what was going on behind the scenes, she stood fully prepared to walk down the aisle. A cappella, I opened my mouth and began to sing.

You are so beautiful, to me.

You are so beautiful, to me. Can't you see?

You're everything I hoped for...

You're everything I need

Kristin, you are so beautiful, to me.[2]

My voice had become her wedding march. She cried as she walked towards me as I continued to sing until she took her rightful place by my side. Her grandfather was a Minister and a General in the Salvation Army (I didn't know the Salvation Army was actually a real army), and he presided over the ceremony. The pastor of my youth (The Rev) said the prayer, and my siblings were all participants in the wedding. We had also written our own vows to say just before we said the "I do's." Following those and the kiss, we turned around and jumped the broom in remembrance of the African tradition when our slave ancestors were not allowed to have weddings. They signified their unions by jumping over a broom.

The reception was held at the Renaissance Hotel near LAX. We had the grand ballroom all prepared with decorations, food, and a DJ. This thing had the potential to become a real party. Everyone ate, drank, and laughed while fraternity brothers sang and stepped. I'm sure that somewhere ex-boy and girlfriends were in mourning because we had officially become Mr. and Mrs. Montell Jordan.

We had our first dance together as a married couple and the song we chose was by a group called After 7 called "Ready or Not." At the cutting of the cake, we skipped the whole "smush a big piece into your face" thing. At black weddings that could lead to fist fights.

Our honeymoon would find us on a cruise to Mexico with about $290 in cash we received during the traditional money dance (where family and friends dance with the bride and groom and pin money on them) during our wedding. On the first night of the cruise we found ourselves investing a portion of our wedding fortune on BINGO, black jack for her, and the craps tables for me. We always seemed to take great risks early on in our relationship, and this carried over into our marriage. This was a gamble that paid off; by 5 a.m. we had amassed over $1500, which allowed us to enjoy the trip with no thoughts or worries of finance. We laughed, partied, danced on tables, rode horses, talked, made love, and for a brief and authentic time, we enjoyed just the two of us, husband and wife. We would soon realize moments like those wouldn't come often, especially with the industry ride we were about to begin.

SEVEN

This Is How We Do It

Once we returned from the bedroom back to the boardroom, we moved full steam ahead into completing the album. Establishing Kristin's role in a music business where women were already at a disadvantage was the initial challenge. This would become magnified once the female manager was also looked down upon as "the wife" and not the businesswoman she had been prior to our vows. One of the biggest errors we would make that would one day return to haunt us was our decision to conceal our marriage from the industry and the rest of the world. True, the industry was different back then. We were advised by our label's A&R people that the fans wouldn't make a star out of a tall, good-looking, unavailable married guy, and Kristin's growth in the business would suffer if she became "Montell's wife." In fear, we both agreed that she would remain Kristin Hudson the business woman, and I would be the single ladies' man, and R&B star. We even came to an agreement that when asked if there was anyone special in my life, I would respond with, "I'm married to my music." Professing my marital allegiance to my music, what would that make my wife? The answer is, *my mistress*. We were unaware of the power of life and death we had in our mouths, and these words planted seeds into the soil of our hearts that would later bear an entire garden of bad fruit that neither of us would ever desire to eat. Behind the scenes, we considered ourselves to be a functional, happily married couple. In reality, I was a growing R&B sex symbol who subconsciously felt rejected by a wife who didn't receive my last name or come under my covering, and she was an uncovered, non-submissive, and independent woman seeking to carve out her own identity outside of me and God. We were Christians, yet we didn't resemble Christ very much, if at all.

Many may not understand how we could consider ourselves to be Christians and enter the music industry and make the choices we chose and create the content we made. The reality is that even though our first album contained cursing, sexual content, and questionable material, we believe God allowed it. That is a bold and debatable statement. My life is the proof. I submit to you that Jesus promised that He would never leave us and never forsake us. And by definition, never means *never*. So when I am doing the right thing, He is with me. This also means that when I am doing the wrong thing, He is still with me, actively working inside me to turn my heart towards making the right choices that won't cause His sacrifice on the cross to be in vain. I believe Jesus knew He would be able to use our testimony we have today by allowing us to journey through the darkness of our choices back then so that the world would one day see that our transformation could have only come from Him. We took the songs from our first album to every church service we attended and prayed for God to bless it and allow our music to reach the world. I don't believe God condoned, endorsed, or approved my content or my methods of trying to achieve fame; however, I do believe He allowed it.

Once the album was complete, there was a huge conflict within the company over what the lead single from the album should be. We had 17 music samples for our Hip Hop street credibility, and multiple rap features from my label mates providing additional endorsement. I made good on my promise to my God brother Shep, and initially brought him on board as a producer and songwriter on the album.

Releasing a new artist in the fourth quarter (end of the year) was frowned upon, and the uncertainty of the single choice resulted in the album release date being pushed back from August 1994 to February 1995. Much of this is because many inside the organization believed "Something 4 Da Honeys" was a strategic choice, which would be followed by the no-brainer "This Is How We Do It" smash. The argument was this: if "Honeys" didn't work, there wouldn't be a second shot for me as a new artist that was already defined as Russell Simmons' rap singer in a climate where rap was not being at all played on R&B radio, or possibly later opportunities for the label for that matter. Following several heated discussions and delays, we all determined to come out guns blazing and introduce "This Is How We Do It." We were taking a huge risk. In essence, we were going all in on the very first hand before any cards were even dealt.

As the holiday season arrived, most of the music business world shut down and radio stations would lock their playlists to include only songs that made their deadline. This meant that any song that made it into the station's rotation prior to the cut off date, or was *added*, would receive a certain number of spins or plays during the weeks the industry was on hiatus.

So as winter approached, Def Jam distributed sampler tapes (CDs and *white labeled* albums) of the songs from their artists to be released in the upcoming year. This was done to stay fresh in the minds of the radio executives just before the Christmas break. Then after everyone returned to their posts in the New Year, a second mailing was sent out again to refresh them of the things they had heard before the break. But something very strange happened with the Montell Jordan song that was included on the sampler.

The DJs who received advance vinyl of "T.I.H.W.D.I" began killing it in the clubs over the holidays. There was a ground swell on the record that was undeniable. Many DJs were spinning the song in their radio mix shows and the spins were beginning to add up. Def Jam had not even officially gone after the record, yet some radio stations that couldn't wait till the New Year to get their hands on a copy had the DJs record copies from the vinyl and began putting it into rotation. The song was in demand that much. This was a unique situation, and we all knew it.

I was a rap singer. It's as though I was a rapper disguised as an R&B artist to assist Def Jam in infiltrating the radio world to gain territory for their hip-hop musical advances. I was willing and ready. During my introduction into the music world, R&B was looked down upon if rap was included in an R&B song. Guest features hadn't become the thing yet, and as a matter of fact, many of the "straight R&B" stations would only play an edited version of the song that excluded the 8-bar rap that I personally did on the song. I don't want to sound like Little Richard, so I will just say that if there ever was an innovative marriage between the two musical styles back then, "T.I.H.W.D.I" is hopefully worthy of mention. Today, rappers sing their own choruses and singers rap their own features. I am currently writing this during the 20-year anniversary of that album and the song's 7-week run as number one on the billboard pop charts. In my heart, the voice I couldn't find back then was captured in a musical style that did not exist prior to that project. My nasal, rap-singing, soulful and playful delivery would become my calling card to one of the biggest party anthems of this century. R&B and rap had a baby back in 1995; it's now 20 years later, and that baby looks like me.

The song would officially become an anthem. They played it in stadiums and arenas, and the song was even licensed out for TV commercials. I remember being the guest of honor at the fabulous Forum for Laker towel night. Twenty thousand or more towels with the purple and gold Laker colors were printed with "T.I.H.W.D.I" and distributed to the fans. Whenever the song was played, the atmosphere always elevated. It was the same everywhere I traveled and remains the same even today. I had no idea (and never could have guessed) that, 20 years later, TV shows and commercials from tax companies and restaurants (Jackson Hewitt, Sonic), from beverages (Pepsi, Mountain Dew) to *The Tonight Show* with host Jimmy Fallon would all continue to reignite a small piece of musical history that would become more famous than even my very own name. Leadership-training guru and personality John Maxwell even has a customized version of the song. Still, when people didn't know my name, they would see my 6'8" frame and recognize me and say, "Hey, you're...you're...This Is How We Do IT!"

Another reason for our great success at radio was because of the customized drops I did. I'm sure I'm probably not the first one to ever do this, but I'm positive that I was one of the first to go to the great lengths that I did for radio. I would re-sing a customized version of "Do It" for almost every radio station in the nation that I visited and added their city in the "south central" part of the song. For some stations like 92.3 The Beat in LA, I literally re-made the song to be an LA anthem. Radio DJs *Sway* and *King Tech* were instrumental in the early development of my song in LA. But New York, for example, didn't recognize LA like Californian's did. So in order to get NY to embrace the song, the lyrics were altered to say, "New York does it like nobody does." Every station in each city I traveled to now had their very own individually customized version of the song. I would even place the air personalities' names into the verse, which would guarantee multiple plays each hour, as jocks never minded hearing their own name in a song. I would roll into the station, get a list of the radio hosts, their show names and surrounding counties, and then freestyle for five to ten minutes until I had rewritten the song. My freestyle rap ability made this method simple and systematic. Recite, record, repeat. This was the formula. I would repeat this action for sports teams and television programs across the nation and anywhere music was played for the masses. I considered myself to be a radio-driven artist, so we (the label and myself) would do everything necessary—or unnecessary—to get airplay.

We had a monster song growing as we headed into 1995. At home, Kristin and I had been married for only six months, but because of the rush of success, we were preparing to hit the road to promote the single. There was no guidebook or instruction manual to assist us in navigating these waters. Def Jam had never done this before with an R&B artist, so together we were figuring it out as we went along.

Radio and touring became the lifeblood of my career. Whereas other artists like R. Kelly had massive radio airplay but always declined radio interviews, I was the opposite. I developed great relationships at radio stations on behalf of the label and my career. Kevin Liles, a radio label rep who would later become the president of Def Jam, once said to me, "If you want to sell a million records, touch a million people." I embraced this theory and signed every autograph, posed for every photo, and accepted every opportunity to become famous.

EIGHT

We're on a World Tour

My first performance as a signed recording artist was at a club in Norfolk, VA, for the station WOWI that had been playing my song more than any station in the U.S. At one point the station was burning the record nearly 130 times a week. In other words, the song was playing almost every hour on the hour, around the clock, and sometimes several times an hour during peak listening times. Virginia was ready for me, as the station had been promoting that I was going to be live and in concert. I, on the other hand, was scared senseless. In my mind I was coming to promote a song, not perform a concert. Something inside me feared I was going to disappoint the fans who were paying to see a concert. I was experiencing the fear of being unprepared.

I was more nervous than I had been in years. I was never this nervous prior to entering the music business, yet the feelings of fear I experienced were reminiscent of those I felt while seeking to gain entrance and acceptance into a college fraternity.

Back in 1989 when I pledged into Kappa Alpha Psi Fraternity Incorporated, no matter how much effort was put into preparing for a "session" with the brothers, they had already decided the outcome: we were all going to catch hell. My line brothers and I studied information to please those in authority over us, hoping our efforts would detour any physical interaction during our pledging activities. This never worked. The fear of never measuring up, along with the resurfacing childhood names of abandoned, bad luck, struggle, and others would all come flooding back to the forefront of my memory.

Now, I was being pledged by the music business and entering a new season of self-inflicted hazing. From that very first show and every show for the next few years, I had to vomit just before every performance, right as my name was being called to take the stage. I'm serious. It was my insecurity of not being able to satisfy the audience. It was about me doing my best and it not being acceptable. To clarify, for nearly 7 years, I had a *bucket* included in my show rider to keep offstage so that I could throw up once my name was called during the artist introduction. For nearly a decade I would not eat several hours prior to show time, as it was easier for me to recover from the dry heaves as opposed to the chunky variety.

That night in Norfolk I performed 4 songs, although I only had 2 songs prepared. I did "Honeyz" and then "T.I.H.W.D.I," which sent the Virginia crowd into a frenzy. As I left the stage, the audience wasn't satisfied. I didn't have anything else to give to the standing-room-only club of drunken, anxious fans who waited around the block to see their new favorite song maker. I went back on stage and began explaining that I was a new artist, and I didn't have anything else when I was interrupted by chants of "This Is How We Do It!" So, I started the song from the beginning and did it completely through, all over again. They loved it even more the second time.

And then they still wanted more. So I did it again. Three times I did the same song during one small concert appearance. I sang that party anthem until the audience was exhausted, and I was delirious. I would later have to learn the art of "leaving them wanting more," but that night they got everything they wanted.

We kicked off the beginning of 1995 with an international tour. With a team of four dancers, Kristin, my music director Shep, and a road manager, we headed out to Europe for a huge Polygram conference in Madrid, Spain. We traveled throughout the UK and spent several weeks overseas. I recall being at an event where Sir Elton John was live in concert in a intimate venue, and in the middle of his set, he paused to congratulate me, on the microphone, as his label mate and on having the number one R&B and Pop song in the USA. Once my single took over Madonna's spot at #1 on the Pop charts, we had made history. It was the first time Russell Simmons and Def Jam ever had a number one pop record. After his compliment, Elton continued into "Benny and the Jets." I can't articulate how surreal that experience was for me; an iconic musical legend had just mentioned my name.

I didn't do any television shows. I had the #1 song in urban America for 8 weeks and white America for 7 weeks. There was no Arsenio, Letterman, Leno, Saturday Night Live, Regis & Kathy Lee, and no television exposure whatsoever. I believe the album was only as successful as it was by the grace of God allowing the song to take on a life of it's own. We didn't do much to help it. Really, we just tried to keep up with it. The label might give a different story, but the truth is, we all knew that I was a guinea pig. I was experimental, and many of the things the Indie record label machine would later learn how to do came from the Montell "T.I.H.W.D.I" experience. I do recall doing almost every radio station Summer Jam and free concert the label could commit me to as returned favors for the spins resulting in the hit record.

Once we did return home from Europe, we began what I believed was my personal 1995 version of the "Chitterling circuit." This was the method the label used with their rap artists; so as their rap *singer*, I used the same template. I often traveled solo or with other breaking artists and was mostly booked by small promoters. We often traveled to smaller and even backwoods cities to do club shows for little or no money, but I gathered ghetto grass roots support and street credibility for my artistry in the process. This was a big thing for the Def Jam brand. I would do strip clubs on their off nights, and even juke joints (very reminiscent of *Harpo's* in "The Color Purple"). We also stayed in the raunchiest motels imaginable, often nervous and concerned about getting robbed by neighborhood undesirables or jerked by the promoters. These were the kinds of places where you could catch crabs from the bed sheets. But I was told everyone had to pay their dues, and *American Idol* hadn't been invented yet, so I sucked it up and climbed on in.

Radio was different then. Without it being said, stations were either being paid to play our records or those running the stations were personally being blessed by the labels. Spins plus sales equaled higher chart positioning. The regional reps for the label also had become local stars in their own right, as they had the access to the artists and rising stars like myself. People were getting paid while I was getting promoted.

The journey had begun. When I pledged the fraternity, brothers would often tell me that although pledging was hard, the real pledging would begin once I actually got into the fraternity. I never imagined that could be true, considering how my butt and head were often feeling at the time. But their words were accurate. I would find the same thing to be true of the music business. My struggle to get into the industry would not compare to the struggle to survive in it. The struggle to be faithful to God, to marriage, and to myself was now in full swing, and fame was only gaining momentum.

NINE

An R&B Group Saved My Life

My first single had been on the airwaves for almost 7 months and was still going strong. The remix had given it new life at many stations as well. As we geared up for the second single release, the song was met with some resistance. It wasn't because people didn't like the song or that it wasn't a hit. Plain and simple, the radio audience still wanted to hear "This Is How We Do It." We went forward and released the "Somethin' 4 Da Honeys" single in August of 1995, partnered with a $720K video from Hype Williams. A ghetto golf classic idea took a wrong turn and celebrities and scantily clothed women scurried for safety as the hood came to the hills. This would become a defining moment, drawing a line in the sand between my rap artist label mates and myself.

We needed a new song, yet it only reached a mid-chart position of about #14. This could be the kiss of death for a new artist, because the *one hit wonder* stigma starts floating around. After releasing a phenomenon like "TIHWDI," the fans and my peers began to look at me with a question mark after my name. It was apparent that starting with your best record did have a downside.

Fortunately, Kristin had a plan. She confided in new Def Jam president, Lyor Cohen, that she wanted to get us on the Boys II Men Tour. She had her eyes set on a big tour for the summer, and asked if the label would provide tour support. He told her there was no way possible that we could get that spot on such a huge tour. There were too many successful acts out at the time all looking for a spot on that bill. But he agreed that if she got it, the label would provide some form of support. God can be extremely funny sometimes, as there was no way we should have secured a spot on that tour. Somehow, she hustled and landed us the opening act slot on the biggest tour in the US in 1995. Boys II Men, TLC, Mary J. Blige, and Montell Jordan.

We began paying our dues. The bathrooms were often our dressing rooms, the pay was minimal, sometimes the performance time was cut short, and often we were sent out on stage early to perform for an empty house as the doors to the venue were just being opened. It was almost a fraternity-like structure where once you joined a tour, you got pledged until you became successful enough to one day become the headliner yourself. We had limited space and about 18 minutes of show time where we somehow incorporated five wardrobe changes into that 18-minute performance. Immediately following the show, we hit the road to arrive early to every city and take advantage of my radio relationships. I would go on the morning shows and ask the fans to arrive early, so that they wouldn't miss their favorite song, just in case I was thrown to the wolves in paying my dues. Consequently, the venues began filling up quicker, with more fans flooding into the arenas early to make sure they didn't miss "This Is How We Do It."

Boys II Men were always cordial and warm gentlemen. Still, I'm certain they were behind some of our staging drama. They earned it. If I'm not mistaken, I believe MC Hammer had broken them in on his tour. They were now the headliners and had earned their rite of passage to induct me.

The ladies of TLC were cool as well. Crazy, sexy, *and* cool. (Sorry, I couldn't resist.) Most of the communication we would have with the group was with Chili, who always was sweet and kind to us. Lisa "Left Eye" Lopez was a special lady too, always playful and full of energy. A few weeks into the tour T-Boz became ill, and the group was forced to leave the tour. They were not replaced. They just increased the performance times for Mary and myself. I was now given 22 minutes of show time.

After another month or so, Mary J. Blige experienced great success with her album sales and exposure and left the tour to go off and begin headlining her own show. She was not replaced either. My fee was raised, I was given more space on stage, and my performance time was extended to 30 minutes. It became the Boys II Men Concert *featuring* Montell Jordan. We would continue to tour with just our two groups for the next 5 months with great success. The longer we stayed on the road, and the more my fame grew, the more I found myself compromising my already uncertain character.

Time and time again my character would be tested. With fame and popularity, I would find that almost anything I desired was accessible. I didn't smoke, but if I wanted it, I could have instantly gotten it. It is an unwritten rule that the artist is always supposed to be kept happy. Drugs, alcohol, or women, whatever the desired vice was, people surrounding the artist could always be counted on to provide. I had two major issues that would begin to manifest themselves in my life and behavior: alcohol and lust. There was no shortage of either of these resources, and each was always made readily available. I entertained and toyed with the thought of having access to them because I had a hidden issue of loneliness that I would later have to identify and deal with. These are difficult words to write, and I'm certain they are difficult to read. But I know that my testimony becomes my strength. Until you see the depths that I sank to, only then can you fully understand from where God brought me. God always provided me with a way of escape, but I did not always take it. I used masturbation as a deterrent to keep me from violating my marriage vows, although at the time, our marriage resembled more of a business arrangement. I was on a moral decline and felt there was no one I could confide in to stop my descent. I hadn't been to church in nearly eight months, and the more fame I gained, the more integrity I lost. On the outside, in the flesh, I appeared to be winning; but on the inside, my spirit was slowly decaying. Fame costs more than most of us are capable of paying.

I maintained great relationships with my Def Jam radio reps in each city we entered. I was the type of artist that didn't mind going to radio, signing autographs, doing phone interviews and station drops, in addition to going out of my way to always remember names of both important and not-so-memorable people. Station programmers, music directors, and office personnel were always fascinated that I would remember the names of people who I had met only once, but upon meeting again could recite the name along with the time and place we met. This was a time when I truly loved radio. I was told on many occasions that two of the best guys who knew how to work radio were LL Cool J and myself because we knew how to make people feel important. And that was important in this game, because you never knew when the office janitor or receptionist could become the station programmer.

Even through all the musical politics and mishaps on the road, Boys II Men and I would come to the end of the road (pun intended) on good terms. I had been paying my dues and had stuck it out for the entire length of the tour. The last night was a show scheduled in Vancouver, Canada, which also was almost the last night of my life.

We had gotten close enough with the guys to be able to plan a practical joke on them for the closing night of our 5-month journey. The dancers planned to surprise them during the show by taking the stage mid-performance and spraying them with cans of *silly string* as they sang the song "Motown Philly." I would join them, and it would be unexpected and perfect.

I toured with these guys for months on end, yet never saw their complete show as I was taking photos, signing autographs and body parts and doing the artist thing. This final night, I was brought on stage where we performed a mash-up (before the term existed) of "This Is How We Do It" and "Motown Philly." It was classic. I had never seen Boys II Men's show before and I was unaware of the pyrotechnic portion of their performance. Once backstage, I barely escaped an explosion where flares shot right in front of my face, and caused me to lean back, startled, on what I thought was a wall. It was actually only a black curtain, which led to a fall off the rear of a 7-foot stage. My hands were covering my ears from the explosion, which meant I was unable to use my hands to break my fall. I literally fell off the stage, backwards, and landed on my head and the back of my neck.

I was motionless. As I looked directly up towards the arena ceiling and black curtain, I realized what had just happened. I knew I wasn't dead, but I also knew I couldn't move. As I lay numb in my murder scene-like chalk-outline position, I thought that perhaps I was paralyzed, considering the way my spine and head smashed to the concrete upon impact. I wasn't dead, but paralysis was a definite possibility. I attempted to execute a simple move like wiggling a finger, but I could not. I was probably on the ground maybe half a minute before Kristin was notified and rushed from the crowd. It seemed like an eternity before the dancers or anyone else was able to get to me.

I could now see and hear Kristin above me crying and yelling for assistance. The dancers were concerned as well, as their employer, friend, careers, and upcoming tour were now in the balance. I could see that the lights inside the main arena had also been turned on as Boys II Men had been made aware of my accident and had notified the crowd. The concert stopped, and *the entire arena prayed for me.* To this day I believe that is the reason I lived.

I had fallen off a stage nearly seven feet from the ground. I barely missed being hit by explosives and was unable to break my fall. For all intents and purposes, I should be dead. Yet once arriving to the hospital, the doctor told me that I didn't have one broken bone. I had only suffered a mild concussion and could expect soreness from the fall. Not one broken bone.

I can only think about how good God had been to me. How else could I have walked away from an accident like that? As I lay there on that arena floor, I felt as though every bone in my body had been shattered, and yet, the prayers of an entire arena found me at the hospital less than two hours later with not one broken bone. As I look back on my life, I'm certain that a divine healing took place, and my very existence today is a miracle. I have to give God the glory for that experience, because only He and I were there to witness it. A minister once told me that a miracle is when God does something inexplicable but chooses to keep it anonymous.

The tour with Boys II Men helped expand my career. In my past, I sang in church for as little as seven people. During my very first tour, I had now gone from performing for 70 people in small clubs to standing before 70,000 people in the Atlanta Georgia Dome. I decided that whether I was before a large or small crowd, I would always give my all. It was like being in a church whether it was packed or empty. When I was singing for God, numbers didn't matter: *70,000 or seven*. I carried this philosophy with me over into the R&B music world, and I would one day be tested on my commitment to this principle. Following the promo tour and the Boys II Men tour, I would start my very own tour as the headliner in the fall of 1995. We would begin to travel around the world.

TEN

There's No Testimony Without the Test

During my first world tour we traveled to Australia, New Zealand, Japan, Bahrain, South Korea, France, Italy, Germany, Switzerland, the UK, and many other places. There was no shortage of compromising opportunities. There were countless cities, arenas, clubs, after parties, temptations, near misses, and drunken nights where I was attempting to navigate this repetitive cycle of becoming famous in front of people on a stage, and then retreating back to the reality of my life where in private, outside of God, I stood as a man who had everything but was worth nothing. I was seeking to build my identity and self-worth from people's adoration and the spotlight. Outside of music, I had no identity. I was fine being Mr. This Is How We Do It—at least that was somebody.

I was pushing the limits of morality, my marriage boundaries, and my character. Sometimes during the video shoots, Kristin was right there, watching. As a manager, she said nothing, but as my wife, it was killing her inside. Speaking out to the label or director about her concerns would have been seen as a sign of weakness, so she held her peace. I felt awkward, but still enjoyed the moments when she wasn't present to see me entrapping myself. I found early on that I was willing to compromise, and this would be damaging to my character. My pride would cause me to do many things out of character.

As we toured, Kristin would fly out from time to time, yet she mostly ran our operation from our home in Los Angeles. It was *the home that Boys II Men built.* We purchased it near the end of 1995 and words cannot explain how fast our lives were moving. This example is best explained by stating the fact I slept in my own bed only 13 times the entire year of 1996.

I always considered myself to be a student of music beyond artistry, and there were many musical icons I looked to for R&B inspiration. As a small kid, I overheard stories from friends of my mom who had attended a Teddy Pendergrass concert, and they spoke of the sensual control he musically presented during his concert. One night I took the stage in Amsterdam, and I remember wanting the show to be sexy, sensual, and exciting in the vein of my soul music predecessors. I wanted to be in complete control of what was going on in their minds and their bodies that night.

During the performance I pulled out a pair of panties that I had purchased from a lingerie store a few days earlier and used it like a handkerchief to wipe my face and head. This drove the women insane. I threw the panties out into the crowd, almost causing a stampede for the red silk prop. I began to make this a part of my nightly performance, arriving to each city to find the local Victoria's Secret or lingerie store and purchase several pairs of women's panties (all sizes—I wanted my larger fans to know they were appreciated, too). This became a regular part of our tour.

Touring with only one album also caused me to find "filler" material to carry the load of headlining my own show. I would have gimmicks where I would bring women up onto the stage and apply lotion or baby oil to their legs or feet. I thought I was entertaining the audience, but in actuality, I was feeding my own fleshly desires.

On one particular night following the show, women had literally surrounded the bus and wouldn't let us leave without me taking some pictures and signing body parts. I was being drawn deeper into the sex thing.

As we traveled back to the hotel with a caravan of cars trailing us (as they often did), I contemplated how I was going to fight off this night's attack. As I sat surrounded by my crew, I received a phone call. It was Kristin.

"I have a question for you," she said.

"What is it?" I responded.

"How do you feel about having a baby right now?" she inquired.

I was certain that this was a trick question because not only had she expressed to me that she didn't want kids on many occasions, I had been on the road as well. She was testing me.

"Well, honey, right now? I guess we both agreed to wait for our business and careers to take off before we had a baby. So, not right now." I didn't want to seem eager although I really did want lots of kids.

"But what if we did, right now?" she inquired again. I had to think for a moment.

"Are you telling me what I think you're telling me?" There was a nervous silence on the other end of the phone. She wasn't sure how I was going to respond after just admitting to her that I wanted to wait.

I then shout out to everyone on the bus, "Hey, everybody, Kristin is pregnant! We're going to have a baby!"

The bus screamed with joy and roared with laughter and congratulations. This made Kristin feel much better as she could hear our supporting cast was behind her in the phone background.

She later told me that she had gone and purchased about 10 pregnancy tests—and   administered them ALL—to make sure there was no possibility of being incorrect. She was so nervous, and I knew that being pregnant was one of the last things she had expected. As we traced back the weeks to see when she conceived, we found that it happened on a night where she had gotten sick just before her birthday in Canada. Apparently the vomiting affected her birth control pills. Although business was booming, we were in store for a different boom. We were going to have a baby.

I personally believe that God knew I was growing weaker, and He provided me with the right motivation at the right time to keep me strong enough to complete the tour without slipping any deeper into the darkness.

Attempting to explain the level of temptation one could encounter in the music business is an impossible task. One evening while touring with a group of rap artists I stepped from my hotel room to hunt for food and witnessed women in towels quickly walking from room to room—they were having sex with one artist and then changing rooms, moving on to the next person—literally all the way down the hall. I quickly lost my appetite and returned to the safety of my room. The point is that this was only one night in one city. This was available every night in every city. There were many times where I would place myself in compromising situations as well, and at that time, I thought I was in a battle with my body, or my flesh, in the area of a desire I seemingly had for sexual sin.

The reality that I would only come to find many years later was that I was actually in a spiritual battle attempting to fill a God-sized hole with manmade remedies. I did not have my life aligned with God, even though I was brought up in church and spoke about God often to others. I learned that you can be in the church and the church not be in you. I knew about God (The Father) and had a limited understanding about who Jesus was (The Son), yet my Baptist upbringing spoke very little of the Spirit (The Holy Ghost). This keeper, or comforter, would later be the power living within me to overcome the strongholds that had me in slavery to sin for decades, even prior to being married. I identified my issue as loneliness, but it was actually the absence of the Holy Spirit. My appetite for ungodly things would continue as I fed what my flesh was longing for, while it was my spirit starving for the only nourishment that can sustain a soul. I thought I was living the life; I was really just dying inside. I lived in guilt and shame for years. I honestly wasn't really living at all, but merely existing. I'm not the only one who has experienced this soul malnutrition, and it's not limited to just famous people either; some reading this right now may have or even currently be experiencing this void I am referencing. If so, be encouraged. I found the way out, and whether you choose to follow my example or not, at least the choice will be yours.

Kristin's pregnancy came at just the right time. Where I failed to be a good husband, I desired to make up for it in fatherhood. We both wanted to be good parents, so for a season we left the music business and became a mom and dad to our coming child. At 12:39 a.m. on June 15th, 1996, Ms. Sydney Alexis Jordan entered the world and our lives changed forever.

The best way I have tried to describe my love for my daughter is by explaining the love I have for my wife. I know that God placed Kristin in my life, and I have grown to know and love so much about her. Her strengths and her weaknesses, her dreams and greatest fears, her hopes and vision for the future as well as her nightmares of sexual abuse as a young girl are all pieces of her. I accepted the entire package. I had only known her since 1991, but knew I wanted to be with her forever. When I would look at our daughter, it was like seeing my wife *reborn* from the very beginning. I was a man, and I had now taken part in creating a woman. And when I held her in my arms for the first time, it was the closest I had ever felt to God.

ELEVEN

More to Tell

I began the New Year with a new home, a new truck, a new label, a new contract, a new publishing deal, a new lawyer, a new accountant, a new album with a new A&R, and a new baby on the way. God had truly blessed me, and although I gave Him some of the credit, He didn't get the glory. My pride would become the driving force within me as I would attempt to prove my worth to the world and myself, and would also become the motivation to begin building a production empire. I felt I had paid my dues and weathered the new artist storm. I was now reaping the benefits of all that I had sown. Everything in my life was new, including a new set of problems I would soon be forced to face.

With the help of an Uptown Records groomed producer named James Jones, we would begin creating my 2nd album. With a hefty budget of $600K and heavyweight producers lined up, we crafted our second musical offering to be more R&B than the first project. James was brought in to solidify me more as a credible artist who could have longevity and surpass the "rap singer" moniker originally given to me by Russell.

The new album had been released, and we did about 33,000 units in the first week. I clearly remember the day my second album was released, because the group Brownstone and solo artist Aaliyah also dropped albums on the same day in 1996. Our single reached the top 10 on the R&B charts but was considerably less successful than the phenomenal first release of "Do It."

Our musical offering to the *Nutty Professor* soundtrack would assist to propel that project to sales of 1.5 million copies, selling 110,000 units in its first week. A month following this release, my second album would hit the stores and eventually become certified gold with sales in excess of 650,000 units. Three singles would also be released from that project, each of which would also be certified gold (500,000 copies). "What's On Tonight" was produced originally by Jodeci's Devante, and reproduced by Shep Crawford with guidance from James Jones. This song sold nearly 700,000 singles. With two successful projects under my belt that included a Billboard number one, several top 10 hits, one platinum album, soundtrack and single, and four gold singles, I somehow still couldn't seem to overcome the "one hit wonder" stigma. Perhaps it was all in my mind, yet even today, nearly 20 years later I hear the echo via social media alluding to the *one hit wonder* references.

On the home front, Kristin had been dealing with some postpartum depression following the birth of our daughter Sydney. I was unfamiliar with many of the symptoms and wasn't equipped to help her deal with a lot of her recovery following the delivery. Although her mom spent a few weeks with us after the baby came home, we eventually were left to be parents on our own. Kristin was eager to get back to work and not be around the baby all the time; motherhood was somewhat overwhelming for her. Since I was completing all that was needed for the album, I wasn't a good support system either. We experienced more tension on video sets as I continued to compromise a marriage no one could see. On the set of the "Falling" video shoot, I was cheered on to fully engage in the sensual pool table scene with actress Sally Richardson, while Kristin watched. It was not a happy ride home.

My production and dance teams were still assembled, and now we were reloaded with hits, videos, records sales, chart position, and tour dates. With only one or two people replaced here and there, we would hit the road again. I can remember Kristin and Sydney being asleep on the floor in the back of the tour bus with me. We named the bus "Big Shirley" and it was formerly used by the late rapper The Notorious BIG. Sydney was barely two months old and was now on the road with us. The bus wasn't working properly, and as we were now in the winter of 1996, we thought the baby would freeze so we slept on the floor in front of the barely working heater to keep her and ourselves warm.

When Kristin left the tour, my personal baggage would return with a vengeance. Following the birth of the baby, sex between us was almost nonexistent. She was uncomfortable with herself and so was I. It is hard to love someone when you don't love yourself. You can't give what you don't have. I returned to manual stimulation as my answer.

I also gained a lot of weight along with my wife during the pregnancy, so I was now more insecure with myself as well.

I had regressed tremendously. I was now experiencing different reactions from radio stations, criticism from journalists as well as fans, and a substantial decrease in success from my first musical outing. I looked to alcohol for comfort. I had been away from church for a great length of time, so my flesh began to crave the things that I felt I wasn't getting at home.

As I continued with the mind battles that manifested themselves in my flesh through lust, alcohol, and depression, we traveled the world again.

The most frequently asked question from people was always "How are you ever going to top 'This is How We Do It'?" In my mind, I had no idea if I could ever achieve that level of success again, so I developed the answer that "If I never do it again, at least I can say I did it once." Although I wanted to experience success on that level again, I became content with the idea that being consistent was just as good. This thought process I subscribed to was partially the label mentality as well.

I remember that during this second album run I was in Seattle, Washington, at an outdoor venue that held about 5,000 people. I had been at the Gorge in Seattle the year prior on tour with Boys II Men, yet now I was the headliner of the show. I get a kick out of the scheduled artist lineup from that tour date. The National Anthem was sung by a young group of white guys called The Backstreet Boys. I was told they had experienced great success in Germany and were about to go for success in the U.S.

They came to my dressing room and introduced themselves prior to the show. They were nice guys, and someone even told me that over in Germany, they used to perform a medley of Montell songs during their stage show. I was flattered. The Backstreet Boys, Soul 4 Real and Montell Jordan. I was the main guy now—and also the main target.

There would be times when I was out on the road and would again be tempted. What began as flirtation with one woman became "harmless" hand holding with the next. After that exchange, it progressed into a friendly hug or close dance with the next. The dance would eventually become a caress or a massage with the next, and that would become something else with the next. You get the idea. With each city, each instance would draw me deeper and deeper into pushing the limits of what I was willing to do. It all would become guilt. I was dealing with being alone, and I didn't necessarily like myself much. I felt better drinking, performing as *someone else*, or taking the focus of attention off me. When I say performing as someone else, I am referring to my inability to identify who Montell really was. I was the cool R&B artist; the non-smiling sex symbol my label execs were designing me to be. I was anyone *but* the faithful husband, father, and man of God that I often professed to be off stage among my closest friends and family.

TWELVE

The Hits Keep Coming

We toured a lot, and the finance coming in seemed unending. Long before the home recording studio had become the "in thing," we booked out entire recording studios, sometimes three and four separate rooms at a time, for weeks and even months. We easily accrued studio costs of $15k-$20k a week, not counting engineering, food, and other equipment costs. We spent hundreds of thousands of dollars recording songs with no placements on artists.

We secured the services of our musicians and producers who would become the "Mo $wang" production team. Our storefront record label would be branded as Mad Money Music, or M3. We began purchasing jewelry and securing publishing deals for these church musicians turned producers, long before any of them had ever achieved a hit record. This process would take place for several hitless years of building our music catalog, developing songwriters, artists and producers, the cost of which was all on the shoulders of Kristin and myself. As long as I had a current record in the market, we all were able to function in what appeared to be a pretty sustainable way of life. I loved this team, and they had become our family. We invested a great deal of money, heart, and soul into the musicians, vocalists, dancers, and entire crew that surrounded us for years.

As we attempted to make the hits, we would also begin to take some hits as well. I had often heard that in the music business you need lawyers to watch your lawyers and accountants to watch your accountants; I experienced this reality in a way that would soon shadow us for nearly 15 years.

The mismanagement of funds on my part led to issues causing me to became delinquent in my taxes. I also trusted our accountants (to a fault) without following up on their work to understand my own finances. This eventually put us several hundred thousand dollars in debt. Funny thing about the IRS is, when a tax debt goes default, they kindly wait and allow penalties and interest to accrue over time before notifying the client of the issue.

Lawsuits also began presenting themselves. We were sued by former managing partners, road managers, people claiming song infringement, people claiming they contributed to songs because they happened to be in the room while the creative process was taking place, producers, and too many others to name. We have probably been sued more than 10 times. Sadly, this often happens to famous people. The rule of thumb is, because it costs more to fight a claim than to settle, fraudulent accusations are constantly brought against entertainers and livings are made by poaching off the success of others. It is another hidden price of fame. We too would end up settling most of the cases that were brought against us, even when we actually were the victims.

I was soon served with a lawsuit claiming that I had stolen "This Is How We Do It" and someone else was claiming to be the creator of the song. These people desired payment from the sales of my albums that they believed to be somewhere in the ballpark of $500,000 and they might be willing to settle for less money with the admission that I stole their song. Many might say, "If you're right, why don't you just fight it?" Well, that's absolutely the same thing we said. If you don't stand for something, you'll fall for anything. I knew there was no way possible to lose in a situation like this, and still somehow they managed to begin plotting and building a case against me. This was personal. My writer credibility and character were being challenged. I decided to fight.

I can never adequately express the stress and distress this legal fight inflicted on us, physically, mentally and financially. By taking on this battle, we incurred a few hundred thousand dollars in legal fees that spanned over a period of 8 years, and all royalties due to me during those years from my album sales were frozen.

Despite the lawsuits and tax difficulties Kristin and I were experiencing behind the scenes, we created our team to become studio rats so that when we weren't on the road, we sometimes would sleep in the studios we secured. We cranked out records for Kristin to shop to the label representatives and built an arsenal of songs that seemed to sit around forever without significant placements. Songs like "Nobody's Supposed To Be Here" and "Incomplete" sat around for several years. Shep and I were dying inside as writers, and the entire team was frustrated that we had hits but no songs taken. We didn't fully understand the season we were in; we were sowing. Planting. Our roots were getting stronger beneath the ground yet we desperately wanted to see the fruit. Many more beautiful, well-crafted, thought-provoking, painful, heartfelt, and personal songs were conceived during this season, but we had to wait for them to come to full term.

If there was any jealousy or deceit amongst our team back then, I didn't recognize it. Then again, we hadn't become successful yet.

With the money we spent at that studio from my company alone, they were able to build new studios and upgrade the old ones. This was prior to home studio and digital recording, so at the time, we had no idea we were investing our money into something we would never see a return on.

The building of our company would lead us well into 1997. I had released an album in 1995 and 1996. I was preparing for my third release in 3 years, but more changes were going on with the label. During my five-album career on the label, they switched distributors four times: from Sony to Polygram, Polygram to Mercury, Mercury to Island, and Island to Universal. Changes like this could be detrimental to an artist's career, depending on the timing of the switch.

I was given a budget of $400,000 to complete my next project. I never received signing bonuses or advances for my albums, and I always used my recording budgets to record. Most of our company and life's survival funds came from touring and publishing.

Our third album was titled "Let's Ride" and featured rap artists Master P and Silk Da Shocker on the single that became my second number one record. That song became the strip club anthem for 1998. I've always believed that the spirit that is on the man or woman creating the music to be consumed is what the person listening will digest. I was spiraling out of control in lust and most of the songs on this third album vividly expressed what I was internally experiencing and suppressing. I was exposing myself in the music under the guise that although it felt real, I was just attempting to create believable stories. My internal spiritual man and my external flesh man were clashing as I went from song to song and story to story on this project.

On each of my albums, I attempted to place at least one or two songs with inspirational value on the projects as an offering to God. This album contained three of those songs. I guess I could have been suffering from *Artist's Confusion Syndrome*, struggling between creating music for the world and music for God. By the way, I just created that term.

Strip club after strip club. Wet T-shirt contest after contest. City after city. Drink after drink. I felt as though I had previously been tested on my ability to deal with temptation from a distance but this time I was thrown directly into the pit of hell and expected to walk through it without smelling like smoke. I was away from home for great lengths of time, and as my marriage had never been the first priority in my life, my insecurities once again allowed my baggage to resurface. We had a smash record in "Let's Ride," and so we headed out to support it and the lifestyle that came along with it. The single would sell more than one million copies and would become my second platinum number one single. The album would also go platinum and two more singles from the project would become gold singles. We were experiencing musical success yet great personal dissatisfaction. I still felt like a one hit wonder, and there were no shortage of haters out there to make me believe it.

I had toured the world for the third time and was still carrying around the same baggage from not only my previous tours but also from my childhood identity issues as well. Following one particular video shoot, a more muscular body double was used to stand in for me in my shower scene. From this, I went through a period of feeling even more insecure about myself, and I was now even growing jealous of the other singers in the industry who were looked at as sex symbols. The guys that took their shirts off and sold their image as well as their music had now become the object of my lust. Meaning, I desired to become them.

In an extreme effort to externally fix an internal problem, I convinced my label to pay for liposuction surgery and have the doctors sign a confidentiality agreement prior to me going under the knife. I looked great a few months following the operation but still took the liberty to eat recklessly and do whatever I wanted to in the absence of the lost pounds. I attempted to hide my struggle in overeating, as though weighing more would cover my sin. Nine months later I gained all the weight back, plus an additional 15 pounds. It's always shocking how the things you always wanted to happen can actually have the worst consequences. That's exactly what happened next. Success and money were about to arrive at our doorstep.

THIRTEEN

Keep Rising to the Top

Kristin continued to shop the song "Nobody's Supposed To Be Here," originally created for Ms. Patti Labelle. Finally, it seemed there was hope that Clive Davis would record the song with Whitney Houston. Puff Daddy also wanted the song for his artist Faith Evans for Bad Boy Records, yet he desired to take the publishing ownership of the song in exchange for a fee. Clive then determined he wanted to record the song with his new artist, Deborah Cox. She would become the artist who legitimized us in the songwriting and production world.

Her song became bigger than "This Is How We Do It," with her single selling more than 2 million copies. She made history, appearing in the Guinness Book of Records as the female with the longest running #1 R&B single in history at 14 weeks. She reached the #1 spot again with her follow-up single "We Can't Be Friends," a duet featuring RL from the group Next. I was originally featured with her on this song, but was removed and replaced by RL. Def Jam wanted to protect me, as they desired me to remain their street credible artist.

We watched the charts religiously each week to see what was happening with Deborah Cox. And Kelly Price. And Lil' Mo. And Tamia. Our producers continued to make songs for Boys II Men and Whitney Houston.

The catalogue of songs we spent building for those few years were now flying off the shelves as everyone and their mother's label wanted a hit like Deborah's. We were blessed to not only get songs placed, but we were producing singles for artists. And between Shep's personal drama and mine, we were able to create some pretty touching stories that would capture the ears and hearts of our listeners when the vocalists breathed life into them. We were finally being recognized by our peers as official songwriters and producers and would even garner a coveted Songwriter of the Year Award from ASCAP (The American Society of Composers, Authors and Publishers). Many of those outside of the music industry had no idea that we were the creators of many of these songs.

The production and signature writing style Shep and I formulated, a chemistry that was based on us desiring to be the next generation Jimmy Jam & Terry Lewis, had taken off and we were able to receive nearly $40K per song we produced. Large portions of label budgets were now coming our way, and for the next few years, the finance that came in was used to afford the elevated lifestyles while the debt accrued to achieve this success still remained on Kristin and me. Publishing companies that wanted nothing to do with our writers and producers in the beginning were now circling the wagons and offering pie in the sky. Many on our team were now beginning to believe that Kristin and I were unfair in the small deals we had provided for them years prior, and that they were now worth millions based on what publishers were telling them. This was the beginning of division that would begin to settle into our team. The production team continued to crank out hits, but tensions were just beneath the surface.

I soon ventured into television, becoming the host of a television series called *Motown Live* for two seasons. I recorded another album, "Get It On Tonite," which would birth my third personal number one hit in the nation. This was my fourth album, and for the first time, I performed my single with LL Cool J on *The Tonight Show* with Jay Leno. LL and I also performed that number one song at the 2000 NBA All Star Game. In addition to another number one hit, this project produced another gold album and two more gold singles. During this period, the Def Soul record label was also blossoming, and I went from guinea pig to the godfather of the R&B/soul division of the Def Jam brand.

I can remember feeling so lonely while I was out claiming to be on top of the world, feeling so far away from home, my wife, my daughter and all the people who really mattered. Many times my choices to abandon my marriage vows had nothing to do with physical attraction. Sometimes it was about lust, but most often it would be about me just not wanting to be alone. Having another person there became almost essential. She didn't have to be a model or even incredibly attractive. I was initially seeking companionship outside of our circle of influence, but the efforts would eventually come closer to home. Most times these encounters were not sexual at all; I was in search of the intimacy I didn't have with God through relationships with people. I was again attempting to fill a God-sized void with man-sized solutions.

As a solo recording artist, I was also the most visible member of our production team. When we would experience song success, my name was often the one brought up, regardless of my level of contribution to the creation of a song. This would begin to cast a shadow over the aspiring songwriters and producers who desired to be recognized for their efforts. For example, whether I wrote 50 percent or 5 percent of a song, when an interviewer read the credits, they would always take the most recognizable name and mention it. On the Whitney Houston/Deborah Cox duet, "Same Script, Different Cast," my contribution was minimal. Yet of all the names listed, I would be commended for writing that record. I now understood why my contributions to our songs were causing negative reactions from my writing partners and producers. Many of the team felt that as long as I was included on the body of work, they would remain in the shadows. It wasn't long before I was being excluded from writing sessions with our team, even though I was still paying for the studio time we secured to create the music.

My pride had me believing it was the anointing on me that afforded our success. As our division began reaching a place beyond repair, Shep reached out in hopes of securing an equal partnership with Kristin and me. It is possible that solution could have salvaged the dissolving empire we had built. Unfortunately, I had somehow forgotten how God used *both* Shep and me as young musicians and vocalists to bless our church's music ministry. He anointed us both. But it wasn't my anointing or his; it belonged to God. I began claiming what was His as mine and would even say to Shep that it was because of God's favor on my life that we were all even there in the first place. Pride does indeed come before the fall. Kristin and I declined his offer and our journey of turning church musicians and singers into super producers and songwriters had seemingly run its course. We seemed to be beyond apologies and solutions.

Our production company continued going through the motions, and I began to search out new writers.

This led me to Atlanta, GA.

FOURTEEN

Exposed

I took a trip to the dirty south in anticipation of songwriting with the hit-making team responsible for Destiny's Child success, Kandi Burress and Shekespear in 2000. I had no relationships or ties to Atlanta whatsoever. Other than performing in the city for the 1996 Olympic games, I had rarely ever set foot on red dirt.

We spent several days attempting to create songs and develop ideas, yet nothing seemed to stick. It was frustrating for us all, so, needing a break, the producer took me on a ride to show me the home he was about to purchase. It was reminiscent of every mansion used to create a rap video, complete with balconies, a swimming pool, and at least a five-car garage. This extravagant home sat upon several acres, and in my mind, I remember my Nana saying to me, "Buy land. God ain't making no more land."

Kristin and I were preparing to purchase a 2400 sq. ft. million dollar home that had no property in Burbank, CA. Now, I was staring at a 7000 sq. ft. home that by our standards was a mansion and cost a quarter million less than what we were about to spend. I knew Atlanta was supposed to be the new hotbed for music, and I was aware that many celebrities lived there. I thought a good reason to consider moving to the ATL was real estate and music business positioning. I had no idea God was strategically up to something bigger than I could ever have imagined. We drove around to look at a few other properties, and with no explanation, I called my wife and demanded she get on the first thing smoking out of LA to meet me in the peach state. Reluctantly, Kristin got on an airplane that same day and joined me down south.

Genesis 12:1-3 is the story of Abram and explains what he was instructed by God to do in order to receive God's promise for his life. I didn't know it, but at the time, I was on a similar journey. I was being separated from the land I knew, the family support system and friends I was familiar with, and the comfort zones I had become accustomed to. I needed to learn more about my destiny. If I was ever to become the artist and leader that I was destined to become, I needed to allow God to re-educate me. During a process like this one, everyone can't come along for the ride. Montell and Kristin would become like Abram and Sarai. There is no other explanation for why we were in Atlanta. The Scripture says, "Go to a land that I will show you." We were there on assignment.

In a borrowed Porsche, we began driving around different subdivisions, just as I had done with the producer. I still never said to Kristin why we were there. I drove up to a property that she would point to; she would hop out, grab the paperwork, gasp in disbelief, and continue on to the next place. We repeated this action for several hours. Back at the hotel that evening, Kristin called her mom and told her we were moving to Atlanta. We never discussed moving, but somehow, we both knew that our destiny was in the ATL.

We returned to LA and immediately began shutting everything down. The offices, accountants, production, employees, everything—we closed shop. We moved to

Atlanta thinking we would build a home on the lake and neighbor with celebrities in a lavish community, yet we somehow felt the need to pump the brakes before fully committing to that venture. We purchased a smaller home in a nearby subdivision where we lived while adjusting from our West Coast exodus. We purchased a 5 bedroom, 3-bath property for $130k—which was still almost equal to what we were considering as a purchase in the Valley. We began attending a large and popular church in GA, and found it was easy to blend in with such a large ministry. On the outside, I still portrayed myself as a faithful husband, yet still, very few industry people knew we were married.

I truly believe what happened next was God's grace. I became exposed. It didn't happen in Hollywood, where everyone could and would witness. I was taken to a place of hiding, where God would begin to uproot the sin and prideful man that I had grown to be. Neither friend nor enemy would have seats to this show. One of our closest friends who knew of my indiscretions could no longer conceal my sin and remain friends with Kristin. I was approached with an ultimatum; they would tell Kristin, or I would. Either way, she needed to know. I knew what I had to do.

After being betrayed by sorority sisters, church members, business partners, company employees, artists and producers, she was about to catch it from the one place she would never expect it. Me. I had to come clean. I knew Kristin. If I told her, I would probably lose everything. But if someone else told her, I would be picking out a "This Is How We Do It" font to inscribe on my grave's headstone.

On September 20th, 2000, just a day before her birthday, I became the reason for the worst day in her entire life. As I began to preface the conversation, for fear that she may take my life, Kristin left the house and went straight to the airport. She returned to LA, seeking answers from our former friends and surrounding cast. Our business supported the lives of nearly 15-20 employees throughout the years, and because no one really desired to rock the boat and risk having food removed from their own tables, no one said a word.

To make a long story somewhat short, she left. She got as much info as she could regarding my infidelity, and I prepared to lose my wife, home, daughter, and possessions to divorce. She returned from California, and we met at the church altar where, to my surprise, God told Kristin to stay and that her life and the life of our daughter depended on it. That day, while lying at the altar, I asked for God's forgiveness. I believe—I know— He forgave me that day. However, it would take me a long time to forgive myself. Pastor Donnie McClurkin's song "We Fall Down" became the soundtrack to this life experience. Literally. After the service Kristin approached me. I didn't know what to say or where to go from that point. Even if God had forgiven me, I was pretty sure that she couldn't.

Kristin told me she wasn't going to leave and that we were going to stay together and work things out. The enemy would not get the glory from what God had joined together. I was beyond relieved, yet incredibly terrified of what was to follow.

It was one thing to tell my deepest darkest secrets to God but to have to tell everything to the woman I loved was, in my mind, a fate worse than death. But in order for God to restore our marriage, our trust, and our family, she would have to know everything. Every single detail, fling, affair, close call, near miss, person, place and thing. I had always heard that everything done in darkness will come to light, and there in my darkest hour, all the lights were about to be turned on. I didn't understand that I was on the road to healing. Confessing my sin to God would result in forgiveness; confessing our sin to one another would result in healing.

We drove for hours down I-20. When I was done unloading my every sin upon my wife, we were halfway through Alabama. I had become free from my exposure, but now my wife was sharing the load of guilt and shame that I bore for several years. I shared the weight of sin I carried for years, and I began to feel lighter. I explained to her my struggles and how I would fall deeper into temptation as time went on. I attempted to express my guilt and shame without expecting her to feel any pity for me. I was speaking to her, but really, I was still searching for the answers to my own questions of why—and how—I had become this person. I spoke of my loneliness and my issues with masturbation. I didn't leave out one person or one encounter. No details were withheld, and every scenario was examined. She withstood this barrage of information from me like a soldier. By the end of this, I physically felt lighter.

Following Kristin's return from LA, the word traveled quickly. I had been exposed. All my ex-employees, artists, producers, friends, and enemies all knew. My fraternity brothers got the news. Close family members, church folks, and label personnel knew that I was an unfaithful husband, and the sketchy details that surrounded the who and how all came out. No one really knew the intimate details other than God, Kristin and myself. In my mind, God had forgiven me, and Kristin was working on it, but I couldn't find it in me to forgive myself.

I stayed at a hotel for a few weeks while she and I both were seeking God regarding what to do next. I spent a great deal of time getting comfortable with being alone with the understanding that if God was present with me, I was never really alone. I began reading my Bible regularly, studying, and meditating on how to be the man God wanted me to become. I began to see that my issues with alcohol, stimulation, lust, weight, and my other insecurities were magnified when I was by myself, and because I didn't like what I saw, I found ways to alter the view of myself. Alcohol allowed me to see myself through impaired vision. Manual stimulation and physical contact allowed me to briefly feel satisfied with myself. My lustful encounters allowed me to see myself as desirable from the point of view the women involved impressed upon me. The fluctuations in my weight were from the heaviness caused by guilt, shame, being biologically fatherless and feeling insecure, also causing me to butcher myself with liposuction twice in an attempt to reach an external solution to an internal problem.

After being separated for a few weeks, Kristin would come and visit me at the hotel where we would talk and pray together. I never imagined or expected that we would be intimate again, but following this trial we had suffered through and endured together, she would open up to me in a way that neither of us had ever experienced before.

I truly believe God showed us that night that He can do anything. There is nothing too big, bad or difficult for Him to replace, repair or restore. There are no words that I can use to express what happened that night, but for the first time ever, we made love the way God meant it to be experienced. It was spiritual. That night while making love, I became more disoriented than on my worst alcoholic binge without ever touching a drink. I was the most stimulated without ever touching myself. I saw Kristin through different eyes, eyes that desired her only. Even the heaviness that I dealt with wasn't present that evening because I felt weightless.

After 6 years of marriage, we finally both opened ourselves up completely, finally arriving at the same place at the same time. It was the closest I had ever felt to heaven. Beyond climax and orgasm (the mental and physical), there is a place that exists where God (the spiritual) becomes involved. Once we tapped into that, we would never be the same.

FIFTEEN

Restoration

This is the most important chapter in this book.

Kristin and I are releasing our first marriage book together in 2016, yet many won't understand why our marriage ministry book is so relevant to couples today without knowledge of the journey from R&B superstar to faithful husband, father, and minister. Without the previous pages, and especially what I am about to write next, you have no context for why I made the step towards becoming unfamous. We believe God doesn't call the qualified, but He qualifies those He calls. There is no degree or pedigree that could equip us the way His spiritual education has prepared us. He called Kristin and me to stand on the frontline for marriage, because only He could restore a marriage as damaged as ours— and yours. Scripture, experience, and the power of Jesus, the living God, are what have enabled us to not only endure, but also thrive together for over 20 years. Some are reading this to have more insight into the story of "This Is How We Do It." Some may be curious of why I left the industry for ministry. Many, unknowingly, are receiving my story because you need hope, as you may see glimpses of your own life in Kristin's and mine. Here's how I got healed:

Friends journeyed from out of state, on assignment from God, to assist me with receiving the Holy Spirit.

Some may think this is odd, or strange, and for quite some time prior to receiving this gift, I thought it was too. But with no shred of hesitation, my life has never been the same since. Prior to yielding myself to God, I had no peace. But after inviting the ultimate Comforter to live within me, I began to experience a peace I never even knew existed. It was so simple, and it was this spirit within me that enabled me to do what I could not do on my own.

That night on the living room floor of my home, James and Caron Jones and Kristin Jordan prayed for me. Kristin was instructed to place her hands on my stomach that night to help me reach my deliverance. As I called on the name of Jesus that evening, not really knowing what to expect, I began the process of *purging* myself. I laid there coughing and spitting up on the carpet, rolling around like a man possessed until a peace came over me unlike anything I had ever felt before. Perhaps you don't subscribe to the idea of demons or evil spirits; all I can say is that whatever was inside of me came out that night.

I'm told that God works through people, and I am convinced that when Kristin laid her hands on me that day, it was a touch from God.

That night I was delivered from the sexual strongholds that had tortured me for years. Not that they wouldn't continue presenting themselves to me, but my desires had changed. No more Vaseline was required. No need to be in the strip clubs. My desires, lusts, need for physical interaction, masturbation, and loneliness began to subside.

God is a spirit. He needs a body to work through. This is why He created man and loves him so much (I am speaking of both man and wo-man, or man with a womb, also known as mankind). When you are in need of a financial blessing, He uses another person to give you a raise, sends you an unexpected check, or opens a door for you to be blessed by another person or entity here in the natural. God has the same desire to provide for our needs in love and relationships as well, especially in marriage.

God desires to touch His people. Not just when He uses a minister to lay hands on someone to heal them but also in something as simple as a parent holding a child. God uses the parent to hold an infant in their arms and give security to the child. God can use a friend or loved one to give us comfort in our time of trouble through a hug or physical contact. When we are afraid, someone can hold our hand, and we feel like we're not alone. I repeat, God is a spirit and needs a body to work in and through. People are touched through music and acts of kindness every day. It was this physical touch through my wife, in faith, that Jesus healed me.

This is how the intimacy was restored in our marriage. I used to see myself as someone committed to pleasing women and tried to build stamina to satisfy and get good reports regarding my ability. Many men often do this. Many women engage in acts to train themselves to be good at one thing or another (within different relationships) as though they are honing a craft or perfecting a skill. This is what happens when we use our own bodies. However, there is something unselfish that happens when we allow God to use us. Yes, even when it comes to intimacy.

I came to the understanding that God often wants to be close to my wife. As her soul mate, God chose and ordained me to be the closest to her. He then desires to use *me* to be the vessel to do His will—if I accept.

What is the result of this arrangement if done properly? When Kristin experiences joy or excitement, God smiles at her through me. When she is in pain and needs a shoulder to cry on, He provides my shoulder for her to use. When she needs a word of encouragement, she can open up the Bible, or perhaps He just wants me to give her the compliment or assurance she needs at just the right time. Sometimes I will pull her close and just hold her tight for no apparent reason at all. I'm not even conscious of my action, and yet God is letting her know that He cares.

I believe God is love. I am in a marriage where we are *in* love, and therefore we are *in* God. When my wife is in my arms, we are so close that we are breathing each other's air; when she's exhaling, I'm inhaling. I savor the moment as though God is there with me, face to face. Breathing life into me. Satisfying my every need and desire. He uses her to do this.

When a man raises his hand and voice in violence to his woman, he's not using his hands and voice in the way God desires him. When a woman constantly nags her husband, argues with him or verbally tears him down, she's not using her voice as God desires her.

When a man uses his hands and voice *for* God, he helps to design the beautiful, strong, and complete woman God desires. When a woman uses her voice, influence, and hands for God, she too helps to design the strong, beautiful, and complete man God desires.

God uses us to continue the process of creation while we exist here on earth. He uses us to give each other comfort in times of sorrow, to share joy in times of triumph, and to experience gratification in times of intimacy. This is why I wrote earlier that God not only restored us but also created something new that had been missing in our intimate interaction. Once it was activated, and *He* was the one who flipped the switch, I feel like I touch heaven each time we make love. And it's not me. It's the "He" in me.

I end these thoughts by asking, "How will you be used?"

True, God had restored our marriage. Now the task was to rebuild it, stronger than ever. We would need to be reshaped and reformed. He restored our intimacy once we both desired Him more than our careers, success, fame, and even more than each other. He was refining us. Pure gold can only be shaped through the intense heat from fire, and even diamonds are only formed from enduring extreme pressure over time. If our renewed marriage would become something for God to show off, He would have to take us through that same process, often known as purification. We were about to experience the fire, but this time, we were going to do it together.

SIXTEEN

After Egypt

I had created numerous party songs, sexually charged records, and believable stories of bravado, machismo, and fantasy. But for the first time, I was prepared to go beyond the surface and get personal. I finally had a real story to tell. Real pain, real betrayal, real forgiveness, real love and real restoration. This 5th album was slated to be the most revealing, open, and honest story that I had ever told.

I was now on a journey to crack the code in how to make the sensual and spiritual worlds collide. I wanted to sing about sensual things, but now through the spiritual lens I was experiencing through the safety of marriage. I attempted to express my transformation in interviews and to anyone who would listen, proclaiming my love for Jesus, my wife, and music, yet I met extreme resistance from the place I least expected it: the Church.

I recall going on Christian television and sharing my heart to the masses, identifying myself as an R&B singer and sinner, and that I was saved by grace yet was still a work in progress. I admittedly didn't have all the answers, but I knew my heart wanted to honor God. I thought I was doing something to honor God by sharing my journey, but this was possibly executed prematurely. Keeping it simple, the responses I got from

Christians were extremely hurtful, judgmental, and uninviting. Sometimes Christians are guilty of making faith unattractive. I began the journey despite the opposition. Here's a truth: there are a lot of musicians, artists, writers, producers, actors, and entertainers who love the Lord. It just so happens that the attitudes and judgmental actions often inflicted by the "saved" people detour those people from seeking God further or even revealing their identities. The truth is, God will not always choose the person we approve of to be His messenger. History has shown us that.

Kristin and I were now attempting to rebuild another production company in Atlanta. We began securing producers and music groups, this time with the assistance of James Jones, the producer from my second album. We recorded hot demos and used our industry connections to plan an event, where we would have talented groups from our new Atlanta-based musical camp, the "Enterprise," prepared to showcase in New York City on Tuesday, September 11th, 2001. Yes, that September 11th. Kristin and I were in Hoboken, NJ, on the day our nation was compromised by the terrorist attack on the World Trade Center. All our artists were actually on planes flying from ATL to JFK that very same morning. The following day, we finally were able to assemble our team following the chaos and tried to create a new plan for our showcase.

We remained there in NY the remainder of the week until we are able to drive back to ATL once the tunnels reopened and we could find rentals. New York would need much time to recover from this devastating attack on American soil, and arguably, the heart of the music business. Our music company never fully recovered from this event either, so our focus shifted on creating my 5th album.

Between publishing deals and albums I took roles to perform in off-Broadway plays throughout the remainder of 2001. It would provide a kind of "manna," or provision, during this time where I was journeying from my bondage (Egypt) and heading for my promised land. I didn't identify this season until long after, but as I look back, I was definitely in the wilderness.

My heart was transformed, and I firmly believe that what is on the inside will ultimately reveal itself on the outside. I hired a personal trainer and got in the best shape of my life as we prepared my most personal album, called "R U With Me?" While completing the project, we taped an episode for a BET show to give the illusion that I was still on top of the world. I had a fabulous life—home, vehicles, material things—all of which were actually *rented* for the taping of this show. This was a humbling experience, but we were setting up the new album and I needed as many visuals out there as possible to help promote the upcoming album. Again, perception was everything.

At the time, I had no idea why God would allow me to go through such a humiliating and humbling experience. I wanted the world to see me prosperous and successful following what He had done for me in my marriage and family. But as I said before, I was prepared to enter the Promised Land and had no idea that I had only been restored and rejuvenated to prepare me for the wilderness. I would soon begin the most trying season in my life and the BET taping would be repeating over and over again, giving people the illusion that I was living good, eating good and the family was wonderful. All the while, I was going through hell. As humiliating and humbling as the taping experience was, that same program would shield me from the world as God continued to break me.

As we prepared to launch the fifth album, we had a beautiful video that featured actress Gabrielle Union and the song was "You Must Have Been," one of my very favorite Montell records. Unfortunately, there was a problem. Def Jam had a formula of releasing Montell projects requiring an up-tempo, radio club banger. This project represented my life at the time, so I couldn't really subscribe to the label idea to go back to the drawing board to create another danceable record.

I was devastated. I had poured my heart and soul into the album, including that song. It was personal. The album represented everything that I had become following the most difficult season in my life (to that point). It was my testimony, and my testimony would become my strength. Many of the songs were not created after I successfully came through a trial, but were written while I was in the midst of the turmoil. The album was honest. The name of the album was even changed from "R U With Me?" to "Montell Jordan," because of the personal content. Without that danceable hit record, the label wanted to abandon the project completely. This became more than just a point of contention but a deal breaker regarding my career with the label. I was too attached to the music of that project as it documented my life and my newfound salvation. There was no momentum or excitement surrounding the project. The writing was on the wall.

I sat in our kitchen a week or so after Valentines Day in February of 2002 as my wife prepared me one of my favorite meals and presented me with a small box and a letter. I was instructed to open the box first, and inside, I found a small pair of baby shoes. In the card was a positive pregnancy test. Sydney was going to be a big sister! This news was a lifeline during this period of drought.

On the ministry front, our name and character were now being associated with unfavorable words, and the mega-church relationship we had once treasured was suffering. It became difficult to focus on praising God while others just seemed focused on us. For several months, we began sending tithes and offering and just watched the services online from home. The ministry was instrumental in assisting us for a season where we needed marriage ministry, yet the combined complicated series of events had us now isolating ourselves. Wilderness.

In March of 2002, I met with Def Jam Records at their request. Going in this meeting felt more business than personal, so we decided we would not share the news with them about us expecting a baby. During that appointment, the label heads told me the news every artist fears: "We're going to have to let you go." I was allowed to keep my website and given $100K (recoupable) upon my exit. I was also given the opportunity to buy back my album, my most personal album ever, for half a million dollars.

My career had come to a screeching halt in the US, yet the wheels continued to spin internationally. My album was still released around the world, everywhere except in America. There was no label support, no finance, no radio push, nothing. My greatest work (in my mind) would go unheard, which, in my opinion, was similar to death. I felt I gave birth to music that was stillborn.

Following my release from the record label, we found our personal internal information somehow began leaking to sources outside of our company. It was more gossip than sabotage, but it still hurt to the core, as the betrayal wound was still open from my past hurts. We had arrived in the wilderness. We released an employee as well as all the producers and artists we were working with at the time.

A little over a month after losing the record deal, I was on a daddy/daughter date with Sydney to the movies. I had my phone on vibrate in the theatre, and I somehow missed seven urgent calls. On April 11th, 2002, I found out that our baby's heartbeat had stopped. I called Kristin immediately, and for the first time, I understood the distinct difference between crying and weeping. I believe crying comes from the heart, but weeping comes from the soul. If I had not been with my young daughter that day, I would have most certainly lost it. (This story is detailed in my full biography.)

As I took inventory, I realized we had lost friends, employees, producers, our second company, the girls group, the guys group, and the male solo artist, in addition to the previous artists with whom we were no longer affiliated. We lost my record deal and the financial stream that accompanied that source of revenue. We lost valuable relationships. I lost my fifth and most personal album. We forfeited the land we hoped to one day build our home on. Due to slanderous words about me, I lost credibility, and after years of teaching others the gift, I lost my ability to create music with my own hands. I lost music equipment to so-called friends. We lost a child to a miscarriage, and I lost a great deal of strength in the process.

We were in one of the driest seasons imaginable.

And in the midst of the storm, we found shelter. God was still faithful, regardless of the circumstances. He still provided for us even in the drought. As I mentioned earlier, this kind of provision is referred to as manna. It was what the children of Israel ate to sustain them when they wandered for 40 years in the wilderness. They couldn't provide it for themselves, and they couldn't save or store it up. Neither could we. It was like daily bread was gifted to us, measured according to only what we would need to endure. Because of this, we were never forsaken and were never begging for bread, as His Word promised. Sometimes people gave us gifts. Sometimes we were invited to dinners at fancy restaurants. Even when we would ask for assistance in an area, we never had to beg and were always accommodated.

We were in the wilderness. Now that God had our undivided attention, we wanted to learn whatever it was that we needed to, and we wanted to learn it fast. God's mercy and grace had sustained us for years following our reaping of what we had sown. And we would ride it 'til the wheels fell off.

We relocated to Lawrenceville, GA, and began living above our means in a really nice neighborhood, just around the corner from our now pastor/producer. My travels internationally sustained our life and a great portion of the new ministry we were a part of. Salaries, tithes, offerings, gifts, and the IRS received most everything I musically scavenged to find. Performances became more of an obligation than a joy. It became work, and more than work, I became enslaved to it. I didn't sell my soul to the devil, but one could argue I leased a portion of it and even rented out pieces of my heart to compromise. I wasn't comfortable singing the same lyrics or dancing the same sensual way. The gimmicks of bringing women on stage to baby oil their legs and create live pornographic imagery for the fans had nearly faded. Going out to perform was simply a reminder of an old life of a man that I had apparently grown up and out of.

Our home would be our refuge during this wilderness period, during which I wrote my autobiography called

Reflections. I also illustrated a children's book that my wife wrote, once again finding another childhood gift that had been lying dormant within me until finding myself separated from music. I also wrote two screenplays and began to tap into the idea that my gift as a writer went far beyond music.

SEVENTEEN

Life After Def

During the seven-year journey through the wilderness, God did some incredible things. He was restoring our marriage and my ability to create music as a producer, not just as a songwriter. However, life as we knew it no longer existed. Bit by bit, we received small glimmers of hope that we would be restored to our prominence in the music business and prove that even without the label, we were capable of achieving greatness. We titled the next album "Life After Def," obviously a controversial name, chosen to spark a conversation about the separation between Def Jam and myself. It worked and conversations were had. In actuality, there was a much deeper meaning involved with the name choice.

Life After Def was more than life after Def Jam. And it was far more than simply a catchy album title. For me, *Def* just became the urban spelling for the word *death.* There was life after the death of the company we built and watched self destruct back in LA. There was life after the many friendships that had to be cut away in order for God to begin tearing us down to make us over. There was life after the death that occurred in our marriage, which was the death of my flesh and new life in the spirit. And there was life after the death of a child as well. Not only were we fighters, but we were survivors. At this time, we found most of our hope in ministry, and prophetic words steadily became the roadmap for us to navigate our way through the wilderness. Most of our resources would be used to provide a ministry salary for our label consultant and pastor, church building, and our attempt to live life like it was financially still 1995, despite the bankruptcy that had occurred in the meantime.

Many reading or hearing this may have experienced that when you begin to earn more money, your lifestyle often rises to meet the level of financial achievement. It reached a point when I was living a borrowed lifestyle; there is no way I could have withstood those seven years without Kristin by my side. We were finally choosing each other over fame, success in the music business, and to some degree, financial stability.

We would experience car repos, property liens, and bankruptcy. Somehow during this season we were able to shoulder the financial responsibility of our overdrawn life and still support the small ministry we had grown loyal to due to their assistance in helping heal our marriage. We began looking to those pastors as the ones who healed us, instead of giving God His due credit. We began to seek getting "a word" from them opposed to getting a word directly from God. During this season, we became more dependent on ministry, as the church and newly formed music company essentially combined. It seemed to work well in the beginning, yet the blurred lines of partnership and pastorship had me questioning my own abilities as a producer. If I didn't like something or didn't agree with a musical direction, it seemed like I was rebelling against the pastor, and therefore, against God.

With my fame fading, I spent many of the next years outside of the country in Europe, Africa, and the UAE in efforts to provide financially for my family, church, and the IRS. The arrangement wasn't ideal, but we were in a season where although we always were the heads of our business, for the first time Kristin and I both were submitting to another authority. We were learning how to serve. As I left and reentered the country, I was constantly recognized, thanked for my R&B musical contributions to the world, and asked when I was coming out with something new. My artistry was seemingly hidden in plain sight as I held on to the promise that I would recover all.

The release of the independent album on KOCH records was dismal and only sold about 3000 units in the first week. This failure was monumental for me and those involved in the project, yet most of the world was unaware that I had even released an album. During this time of travel and stage plays, Kristin and I agreed that our marriage would be our first priority, so it was not possible for me to be anywhere too long without me returning home or her and our daughter coming along as well. The only real bright spot of 2003 was the birth of our son, Skyler, on September 21st. God blessed us with a son following the loss of one the previous year. 2003 also presented another acting role opportunity for me in the release of the film *The Fighting Temptations.*

The next several years found me dying to myself. I can recall one day when our pastor/producer suggested I was entering a season where I would no longer be a successful recording artist and to focus my attention on strictly producing for other artists. In this man-to-man conversation, I was devastated and in disbelief that the journey I had been on would not end with me returning to fame and fortune. Once getting alone with God, I can remember angrily ranting to Him, "How can You do this to me?" Although so much had been restored in my life, I still didn't understand my identity. I thought what I did defined who I was. I was an R&B singer, songwriter, actor, and producer. Without those things, I didn't know who I was. God, in His funny (and not so funny) way of helping me find myself, designed ways to let me find out who I really was. He continued to allow those things to be taken away. Fame. Career. Songs. Music catalogue. Fortune. Notoriety. I felt like the place known as *rock bottom* must have had a small secret compartment beneath it that my life had somehow discovered.

In 2005 we experienced a house fire that destroyed everything we owned, with the exception of some family photos and the clothes on our backs. Only a small portion of the garage was salvaged. Our home, along with two others beside it, was completely consumed. Every award, accolade, and material possession we had ever owned during our lifetime all went up in flames. We detail this event in *This Is How We Do It! Making Your Marriage a Masterpeace*, as it was a defining moment not only in who we were as a family but also in who we would become. Through this devastating tragedy of losing everything yet keeping our lives, we learned a new value of losing your life in order to find it.

Up until this point, I was more enamored with my gifts than with the gift-giver. It took an amazing and difficult wilderness journey for me to understand my identity was never in music, but in Christ Jesus. In other words, I thought music defined me. I thought music made me. I had to be removed and detached from that world, the world of fame, in order to really understand that no one is designed to carry fame. It was only through the beginning stages of becoming unfamous that I began to find out who I truly was.

We soon decided to relocate from our subdivision into a miracle rental in a new neighborhood following the fire and a brief stay with relatives. Meanwhile, the world around us continued to unravel, yet somehow, our family unit began to solidify more than ever before. Without the material possessions and famous lifestyle, God began to speak to us all over again. Things were changing. We began hearing from Him again. Or perhaps He never stopped speaking at all, and I had just become more content with hearing what I wanted to hear. Anyway, I had finally come to understand who Montell Jordan really was, without fame, finance, or a hit record. I was a husband to Kristin. I was a father to 3 kids after the arrival of Christopher into our lives following over a decade of prayer. I was committed to the belief that the local church is the hope of the world, and I served there. I was a son, brother, and friend. I began mending relationships with all those in our life who had wronged us or we had wronged. Kristin and I had a list of 87 names that God instructed us to write down and, one by one, go back and ask each and every person for forgiveness. This task was difficult to execute with people we had wronged yet tremendously more with those who had wronged us. We had to go to everyone, even the producer who we felt wrongfully sued us, and ask for forgiveness. Some of the women we allowed to breach our marriage (who began as friends and employees), we went back to them, both Kristin and me together, and asked them to forgive us. Every situation, circumstance, issue, good relationship gone bad and bad relationship gone worse, we approached them all to repent. This was a near-impossible task, and honestly, we saved most of the more challenging repentances until the end. But we did them all. In most all the cases, we not only freed ourselves but also presented an opportunity for the other party to receive freedom. Many of them didn't even realize they were in bondage until they experienced the freedom of forgiveness. There were a few who didn't desire to forgive us, and it grieved us greatly that we had damaged them beyond repair. God was offering them the opportunity to heal in this process, yet we learned not everyone desires to be healed.

Seemingly lost and tucked away in a nearby neighborhood, without the impressive home with a movie theatre and all the status and thrills, we began to find our family. Monopoly and other family board games replaced the electronic world that consumed us, and the tragedy of the fire not only burnt away our materialistic strongholds but also the unhealthy relationships that had attached themselves to us. In a way, we were being purified. We were being refined, a process that only happens by passing through fire. Little did we know there were still more situations heating up beyond the current oven we had just walked out of.

The most valuable lesson I learned during this time was that music didn't define me; I defined music. Music didn't make me; I made music. This revelation meant that if I never picked up a microphone again, never stepped on a stage again, never had a hit record again, or never was recognized for my name again, I was still invaluable to God. Beyond what a music chart reported or label representative said, I am priceless to Him, my wife, and my children.

I'm reminded of an interview I watched where a famous comedian actor named Tracy Morgan was on television, visibly broken. He had suffered a tragic accident that left him incapable of continuing his career as he had known it. He wept before an audience of fans and the host of the program because following the accident, his comedic timing was no longer in sync. He felt his fans would move on and he would not be able to recapture them before they had forgotten him. In an effort to console him, the actor beside him assured him everyone would wait. I watched his brokenness and relived my similar experience of hoping my fans would await my return rather than moving on to the next big R&B artist. He, along with many others (myself included), placed value on what he did to define who he was.

I would later hear a great mentor say "without Christ I am nothing, I have nothing, I can do nothing." It was not until I came to this realization that I learned how Scripture instructs us that the only true way to find your life is to be willing to lose it. More than praying for Tracy's ability and career to be restored, I pray his value is identified outside of his gift. I realize "unfamous" is not a word; I'm reminded of this with each keystroke that attempts to make me spellcheck what I am sharing in these pages. I also understand that although it may not be an actual word, it is an actual occurrence, and many of us are experiencing the journey of becoming unfamous without even knowing it. After all, it is the road less traveled. Outside of music, outside of comedy, outside of Hollywood, outside of fame, prestige, wealth, notoriety, material possessions, career, occupation, job title, salary, reputation, and everything that we humanly place value on is where our value actually lies. Who we are is not based on the list of what we do. What we do should be based on who we are, a realization that simply cannot happen outside of Christ. This is the greatest tragedy life holds for any of us: never realizing why we were created and not connecting with the One who created us. I am constantly reminded of this truth, even to this day. The draw of fame is like moths to a flame, becoming the default addiction for those who have tasted success.

EIGHTEEN

A House Is Not a Home

While we were still in the midst of the wilderness, our home was slowly being rebuilt, and more importantly, our family unit was being restored. The insurance covered most of what had become ashes, and we truly came to understand how worldly possessions might actually have owned us more than we had ever owned them.

We sifted through nearly 10 years of receipts for purchases that had seemingly defined who we were. The brown snakeskin jacket I wore to the Soul Train music awards, the black python coat I wore only once in a music video...I was faced with hundreds of thousands of dollars for garments I had only worn once, as fame dictated I couldn't wear them again because I was seen and photographed in it on someone's red carpet somewhere. I'm not certain how much real estate we could have invested in, or how many children we could have supported and fed with just a few items I had custom made over the previous decade, but I'm sure it's a lot. Surely the insurance company must have thought we were absolutely insane upon receiving our claim, yet even with the misappropriation of funds throughout the years, we did manage to have an account and receipts for all that we spent. We used most all of the funds to rebuild what we thought would be our dream home.

We constructed every inch of the new home to our exact specifications. Every detail, down to the basketball court no one else had in the entire subdivision, was approved. We took black markers and walked through the construction site and marked Scriptures over every doorpost within the entire home. We wanted our home to be a place of peace and prosperity, and we felt like surrounding ourselves in the Word was the best way to accomplish this effort. Approximately five months following this amazing tragedy, we found ourselves resting in our newly reconstructed home, fully furnished. But our house was still not a home yet. The famous life we used to live was still MIA, so we once again we sought to fill the void.

We became heavily involved with a music-based multi-level marketing business opportunity, and my past music fame seemed to be an asset to the organization. This allowed us to move more quickly within the structure of the company, as it would benefit them to have a Grammy-nominated recording artist validate their product. Through this organization, we formed friendships and made alliances with business partners that seemed to be the next progression for our music and management careers.

In my autobiography, I share that during this dark period in our lives of awaiting deliverance from the wilderness, Kristin and I walked through another one of the greatest challenges either of us would ever imagine facing, yet again. Our marriage was tested once more with an infidelity. This time, it would be my wife entangled in the relationship. Here's a glimpse.

The perfect storm of my personal depression, musical regression, and career digression all were worthy contributions to Kristin seeking refuge in conversations, emotional relationship, and friendship outside of our marriage. My insecurity also played a huge role in one of the most defining moments of our marriage. The enemy also played his hand in reminding her of how I had hurt her and breached our vows years prior, and that I possibly deserved betrayal. The short version of this experience is that she would seek comfort and friendship in someone close to our family, and this would lead to an affair. It began as emotional long before it became physical. Following the encounter, they both realized it was not what they thought it was and decided to continue on with just their friendship and keep the incident a secret. Kristin was prepared to take this encounter to the grave with her. The interesting thing about hidden sin is the side effects are consuming; guilt and shame just kept eating at her, both internally and externally. Our sex life was infrequent, and when we were intimate, she would sometimes cry. I didn't know what her diagnosis was, but I was aware of the symptoms.

This abnormal behavior continued for a few months; I began praying for my wife. Sometimes it's far easier to pray for others than for ourselves. The Lord shared with me that Kristin was holding onto something that would consume her if she were not allowed to release it. God promised me that if she could forgive me for my multiple acts of indiscretion, He would strengthen me to offer the same forgiveness only found in faith. I didn't fully know what I was asking God for or what I was getting myself into, yet I did know living life in guilt and shame wasn't really living. I had experienced this for years and loved her enough that I didn't desire her to suffer in sin like I had. God prepared my heart to hear whatever she would share with me, if she were ready and willing to be free. For years I never fully understood how Kristin was able to forgive me following what I had done to her. What I didn't know was that Kristin never fully understood what it felt like to be on the receiving end of forgiveness after hurting someone. We were now living out Scripture, that those who love much do so because they understand they have been forgiven much. It was only through Jesus that both she and I endured this tragedy and allowed it to become our testimony. We were being prepared to experience giving to and receiving from each other the grace and forgiveness that Christ extends to us.

I remembered many years prior while standing at the altar of a huge church in Atlanta and having the opportunity to confess hidden sin and repent before my wife with thousands of other men and their wives. I rejected the chance due to pride that others would see me and know I was unfaithful. Pride allowed me to stand before my wife and before God and reject the chance to repent and be free. I was now preparing to present this same opportunity to my wife without the surrounding cast of couples or the sermon, and with only the altar of our bedroom before us.

Only those who have experienced hearing the admission of an indiscretion in marriage can identify with the weight of the actions accompanied by the words. The swirling questions, the desire to know details without really wanting to know the details, the insecurities, the anger, the sadness, the fear, the betrayal, the devalued self-esteem, the passing and acceptance of blame, and at least a thousand other thoughts and emotions flooded to the forefront of my mind. Only God can turn a crazy twist of fate into a test of faith. We were now both experiencing what neither of us could previously comprehend. Kristin was prepared to take sin and shame to the grave, but instead, she chose freedom. What was absolutely devastating and should have been the end of me, and the finish line for us, once again became the starting point for God's miracle-working power.

With strength and humility, Kristin made her confession and repented before God and myself. From experience, I knew the greatest challenge before her would be to forgive herself. There was nothing in me that desired to experience what she had gone through, but I knew the weight of hidden sin and never wanted her to endure that silent suffering, even at the expense of exposure to the receiving end of infidelity. We had seemingly been broken, rebuilt, and then broken again. And amazingly, divorce never was even an option.

I absorbed as much pain as humanly possible. I resolved in my heart and mind that I would forgive my wife but I could not and would not forgive the family friend who was involved. I was hypocritical, choosing who would receive my unconditional love. Many years prior, I had experienced carrying the guilt and shame and unforgiveness around. In allowing Kristin to relieve herself of these horrible things, I placed myself back in the "victim mentality" world I was so familiar with. But this time, God had a different plan. The same way we are not built to carry fame, neither are we designed to carry the weight of our sin. This time we were being groomed to accept a freedom that neither she nor I could ever pay for.

As a songwriter, I have always attempted to effectively express the truth and power of words into harmony with melody and music. Here on these pages without melody or music, I prayerfully present to you the greatest words of truth and power that I have ever expressed. *The power of Jesus Christ healed our marriage.* Whether you believe this or not makes it no less true.

One of the greatest life lessons I have learned is that anything and everything of value has never been about me. The journey of "This Is How We Do It" and our rise to fame actually has very little to do with our success or failure in the entertainment industry. While we were seeking success, God was providing access. What does this mean?

Today, we have access to superstar recording artists, musicians, Hollywood film stars, television actors, radio personalities, world-renowned athletes, magazines, and social media outlets due to one hit song we recorded over 20 years ago. In each of these areas, marriage is not revered or celebrated above individual achievement. Kristin and I could not in good conscience experience the miracles we lived and not share it with others who need hope. We were searching for hope in a business that we loved but that could never love us back. Our marital trip to hell and back to now experiencing heaven on earth is something all people, famous or not, need to know is accessible to them.

My confession to you today is that this book is not about my R&B artistry but about me learning that fame will never satisfy like Christ does. I am now preparing the way for others who will eventually come to the same realization, hopefully before their lives are too worn or devastated to recover. Not many will choose faith over fame. Not many can choose forgiveness over infidelity. Very few will choose revelation over relevancy. Kristin and I now have a unique opportunity (and mandate) to reach back into the world of entertainment—from the spectrum of successful millionaire entrepreneurs and business moguls to everyday working men and women— and share the good news that hope is accessible to all who desire it. This hope is only found in the one who designed us, gifted us, and purposed us. I have more peace and significance in my life now than I ever had while famously traveling the world with the number one record in the nation. The music I created may have altered the industry for a season, but my life in ministry can alter the legacy of saved marriages that result in saved families that ultimately impact this world for a lifetime; God establishing His influence through me has been worth far more than a few hit songs.

Perhaps this chapter is not for you. But if it is for you, the husband, wife, father, mother, actor, entertainer, famous personality, athlete, or any person who recognizes through our transparency that our life story and experience are for you, thank you for making the most painful parts of our life worthwhile. When I finally recommitted my life to Christ and was publically baptized in 2008, it was because I realized that if Jesus had the opportunity to rethink agreeing to be crucified, and I were the only one who would be saved by His ultimate sacrifice of love, He would have done it all over again—just for me. That makes me kind of a big deal. And in efforts to resemble Christ, Kristin and I both agree that we would endure the crucifixion of our careers for the resurrection of our marriage all over again, knowing that you received the hope you needed to trust in God and have faith that you too may be resurrected in the areas of your life that feel buried. That makes *you* kind of a big deal.

So Kristin and I have experienced walking in each other's shoes, perhaps even yours. In our case, we had different circumstances but with an identical outcome. In our weakness, Christ shows Himself strong and restores us. Many years later, He would even empower me to forgive the friend involved in the marital breach and bring healing to him as well as myself from attempting to withhold that area of my life hostage. Through the power of Jesus, we both were able to forgive those who breached our marriage, and we believe with everything within us that you have access to that same power. This is the purpose for this book.

Luther Vandross (RIP) once sang the words, "A house is not a home." He was, in essence, suggesting that things are not always what they seem to be on the surface. There are some pretty big houses in the entertainment business but not many of them are homes. Kristin and I have been preparing to begin unveiling the "fake it till you make it" façade that keeps our marriages in bondage to our own sin and selfishness. The next release from Montell Jordan will not be a musical album but another book co-written by my wife and myself titled, *This Is How We Do It! Making Your Marriage a Masterpeace.* We're so excited for our first ministry project, set to be released in 2016. You may get this book and support this effort now by going to www.montellandkristin.com.

NINETEEN

The Call

With the new home and new perspective, we set out to jumpstart my career and experiment with new ideas and business ventures. Our marriage had been miraculously renewed as well and we were now prepared to hit the ground running toward the comeback of a lifetime. There seemed to be a resurgence of interest in artists from the '90s, and with the hit career and fame we once had both before the microphone and in the business world, we defaulted to return to the hustle of the industry basking in the afterglow of our newfound enlightenment. No opportunity went unchecked. We still had years of bankruptcy drama we were entangled in and could feel the years of strangulation taking its toll, even though other areas of our life were being restored.

We held on to the prophetic word that we would receive double for our trouble. We built an arsenal of film scripts, children's books, and music that we hoped would lead to our next big break, subconsciously desiring to be famous again. We began shooting episodes of a YouTube program called "Montellevision," a venture we hoped would land my family a reality television show. We recorded what we believed was the hottest album of my career.

We were working on these projects behind closed doors, not recognizing they were doors the Lord quite possibly had shut. We transitioned from the prophetic ministry we served for seven years to where we felt the Lord was leading and directing us for our next season in life. During a concert trip to Tennessee that summer, we experienced our ministry and music worlds becoming uncomfortable. The blurred lines of my prior artistry and present submission to the pastor caused a few awkward moments that were a foreshadowing of others to come during a gospel-like concert before a secular music audience in a mall parking lot.

We returned home and over the next several weeks, our relationship with our leadership became more distant, reaching a point where we had almost no contact other than conducting the services for the weekend. It had reached a place that was so unhealthy and so uncomfortable that we functioned strictly out of obligation. In hindsight, we believe God knew both Kristin and I would never leave due to our relationship and loyalty to the man and woman who had helped heal our marriage many years prior. But He reminded us that it was not they but He who had worked through them that produced the healing. We were honoring their gift more than the one who gifted them. Second, He reminded us that He alone had recently healed us of our latest marriage situation, and no one in the church—pastors included—were aware that we had even experienced that tragedy, and we made it through. God was enough, and if we continued to look to a man or woman to see and hear from God, we would never fully receive what He had for us. Many members not close enough to us to understand how and why we came to the decision to change our church home viewed this as abandonment or an act of treason following the years of life we invested in the ministry. Despite what may have been said or thought about our departure, we have always loved and appreciated what God did for us there; we also know we were released and allowed to depart in order to receive what He had in store. In reality, we remained far longer than God had instructed us, yet loyalty to the men and women in ministry we loved dearly caused us to stay longer. God allowed us to get uncomfortable so we would begin to seek out what He desired for us. We experienced our last Sunday by serving in every area of the church, and after the services ended, we did not look back. It was not easy and it hurt tremendously. At the same time, it also felt like we were free to experience ministry in a different way, if we were open to it.

In 2008, a week following our departure, we began attending Victory World Church in Norcross, GA, and a few weeks after that, my entire family, with the exception of my youngest son Skyler, was baptized during a Wednesday evening youth service called Fusion. In efforts to take a breath from the leadership roles we had in our previous church, Kristin and I began serving in the children's ministry at Victory. Funny enough, only a few weeks into volunteering in the new church, we were promoted to heading that part of the kids' ministry. There's no real need to explain in detail how we knew we were at home. We just knew.

I was still an R&B recording artist, traveling internationally on mini-tours overseas in efforts to financially support my family and remain relevant in the music business. We were in a new home, but we were in tremendous debt. One day the repo man visited and took back the convertible BMW from our driveway. Kristin even had to go outside in her robe to ask the person to at least allow her to take my things from the car before they took it. I flashed back to being a small kid standing on the front porch of our home in South Central Los Angeles. My younger brother and I were restrained by my dad for wanting to attack the guy who was repossessing our car from our driveway. He told me then that the car wasn't ours. I now realize that the house wasn't ours either. Back to the present day, the car being towed away was not ours, nor was the home we were currently standing in front of. The borrowed lifestyle is deceiving and even enslaving. I had to figure out how to make ends meet as I remained loyal to completing prior financial obligations and enduring the relentless pursuit of the IRS to have access to what I didn't have and what I may have in the future. This was a different kind of slavery.

Throughout the world there were girl group and boy band covers of my song that would keep differing versions of the music in rotation, reminding people that nothing compared to the original. I continued in the wilderness, awaiting the opportunity to return to the public eye and my adoring fans, which I thought were patiently awaiting my return to the spotlight. I traveled with great road managers throughout the years, and during this season, my right-hand man became more than a friend, road manager, soundman, and security guard, but also became accountability for me to remain faithful to my wife. He helped deter the sexual advances that didn't seem to go away but actually became greater as my commitment to God, Kristin, and my family became greater. Community and accountability are invaluable.

A few years prior, we signed to an independent label deal for the release of an album titled "Let It Rain," resulting in us being on the receiving end of an industry scandal that mirrors the horror stories told about the business. This small company preyed on our spiritual and personal investment in the project, and even despite

Kristin's disapproval (who went kicking and screaming down this path with me), I did the deal. *They were who she told me they were.* They succeeded in releasing the masters of that album online without ever manufacturing any tangible product, paying any producers, clearing any songs, providing any royalty statements or accounting for any finances they received. I never got the backend of the deal, but more appropriately, we got back-ended in the deal. (Are you picking up what I'm putting down?) Relationships with writers and producers were nearly destroyed beyond repair, and we looked as if we were doing something underhanded. We fought to have them take the project down, only to have it return after some time.

At the time, online distribution was growing and there were really no procedures to warrant against anyone putting musical works on the Internet or recourse for what to do once the breach occurred. That album is a reminder to me that listening to my wife, even when I don't desire to hear the truth, is a key to our success together. It would take years for me to forgive the owners of this company, but I have. To this day, they still benefit 100% from everything the project generates; still, I forgive them. I have never spoken out against them or said their names publicly, and I take responsibility for my lack of discernment in who they were. I will offer this suggestion as a public service: research the Montell Jordan album *Let It Rain* that "released" in October of 2008. Simply put, consider doing the opposite of what I did.

In efforts to recover from this musical tragedy, we used the remaining portion of 2008 and all of 2009 creating what I still feel was the hottest album of my career. To this day, I go back and listen and realize the potential the project had. Kristin began taking music meetings to shop the project, and there was great interest from labels and private investors. The complete package of a possible television series and hot album piqued the interest of many influential industry movers and shakers at that time, but we somehow kept experiencing the most random instances, and subsequently, the deals would fall through. An investor completely disappeared following months of planning and strategizing. A&Rs who loved the project would lose their job or authority to sign a deal. We spent an entire year focused on maintaining fame and reclaiming relevancy to no avail. There were at least six specific instances where we thought we had a deal in place, and each of these opportunities would become completely nonexistent. In January of 2010, we decided to take the matter into prayer during a 21-day corporate fast the church hosted each year.

The Lord spoke to Kristin during the fast (which for us is a time of no eating or sex in consecrating ourselves to God) and told her that we would not get a record deal, and instead, we would be entering ministry together. Like Sarai in the Bible, I believe Kristin may have laughed at God. She knew I loved Jesus and church, but ministry was the farthest thing from my mind! She appreciated God for sharing that revelation with her, but respectfully, she went on to tell Him that if He wanted me to know this He would need to tell me Himself. Kristin knew how hard we were grinding towards being famous again and had previously experienced my response to what my life looked like from the last encounter hearing that my artist days were over. She didn't want a repeat of that on her own hands so she remained silent. For several months, we repeated a cycle where door after door continued to close. I became more and more frustrated and confused at how we could finally have figured out how to live a life serving God and each other and produce a hot album, but we couldn't seem to get the break we were looking for to return to the business. Perhaps we thought we were equipped to do what we needed to do to reach success again, yet we were not enabled to do what bigger things God desired for us to accomplish. Six months into 2010, our family again went on a personal fast—this time outside of the church—for another 21 days seeking clarity from the Lord.

I remember waking up early one July morning from a dream and being in disbelief with what I experienced. I didn't even share this information with Kristin until later that day. I approached her and said, "Babe, I had the craziest dream last night. I felt the Lord was telling me that we were not going to get back into the music business, and we were supposed to lay it all down and follow Him." I was awaiting a correction from my wife that I was indeed crazy, but instead she looked at me with this "I already knew that" look on her face. I was actually providing the confirmation to what was shared with her six months prior.

That was the moment when both of us knew that we were being called into ministry.

TWENTY

The Response

I'd like to tell you that upon hearing I was being called into ministry, I rejoiced and was prepared to answer a lifelong dream spoken over me from my childhood. Honestly, the exact opposite happened. I became angry with God.

Our new church had embraced our family and my past fame didn't seem to leave anyone star struck or create any awkward fan moments. We would come and go, serving in the children's ministry, and I was occasionally asked to join the worship team on certain weekends. It was actually perplexing to me that despite knowing who I was in the R&B music industry, the church allowed me on the platform. I believe the leadership at Victory saw in me what I didn't see in myself at the time. God revealed to them that I was a worship leader before I ever knew I was leading worship. To some degree, I was a slave who didn't desire to be freed. I was traveling the world out of obligation rather than opportunity. I returned from my travels feeling defeated, only to be grateful to get back to the church where I could get replenished and revived and feel free. I somehow believed that doing what I had done before would fulfill God's promises to me. This is why I continued to go back out, time and time again, doing the same thing and expecting a different result. Insanity.

We were tithers, giving a tenth of everything we earned. We gave generously in offerings. We served in children's ministry and were even working closely in rotating to serve the 20-30s young adult ministry pastors as assistants during the midweek services. We attended church faithfully on the weekends, except when I was out of town in concert or overseas attempting to make ends meet. Our marriage had been restored following the affairs we both encountered.

I was now processing that God was asking me to lay everything down. I didn't get it. What do you mean by *everything*, God? We don't have anything anymore! There's nothing left. What else could possibly die, or better yet, be sacrificed. You see, laying it down would mean I was responsible for the death of it. I didn't have enough faith at that time that the God who raised Jesus from the dead was capable of raising my career from the grave. What little remaining fame I was holding onto may have appeared lifeless to some, but to me, it was the lifeline to the only life I had ever known, or at least could remember.

I remember asking God, "If I were to lay it all down, what would I do? What kind of music would I make? Would I be accepted as a gospel music artist? What would I become? And why me and not someone else?" I immediately defaulted to the Def Jam records mentality instilled in me that I was a party artist who only created chant-worthy, up-tempo club bangers and stadium anthems. I got some of the answers to these questions during a brief visit in Tennessee with some friends who had been independently on the Christian music scene, Beckah Shae and Jack "Shock" Shocklee. We would meet at a Starbucks nearing the end of summer 2010 in what would be a crossroads moment for me.

Kristin and I shared with them how, during two separate fasts on two separate occasions, God spoke to both of us separately to confirm that He was orchestrating our exodus from the music business into ministry. I shared my frustration with them about how after all the righteous living we were now doing, we expected God to make good on His promises. When Beckah asked me how I felt about being chosen by God, I remember my response was lackluster at best. "He's God. He's going to get what He wants. So I really don't have any choice in the matter because He's going to get what He wants anyway. I might as well just do it."

This was the attitude and quite possibly my exact words to her. I watched her face almost burst into tears upon hearing my words. Beckah Shae passionately began to correct me. "How could you say that?" she asked. "Don't you ever say that! God chose you. Don't you get that? The creator of the universe chose you! Don't you realize how valuable that makes you? He could have chosen anyone, and you could have been passed over—but He called you!" As those words began to beat against the tough music business and church-hurt exterior both Kristin and I had built around our hearts, the thought entered my head for the first time, "If I did take this leap of faith, what would it look like and what would it sound like?"

Driving back to Atlanta from near Nashville, something that was seemingly dormant in me was awakened. I called Shock from my car and put him on speaker. I had a beat inside that needed to get out. I beat boxed it over the phone and shared the initial idea that it could be something played in stadiums. Even the organ-like sound played during baseball games could be incorporated into the track if the right melodic pattern was created. He took the idea and began producing the song. There was no record deal. There was no ministry. This was just an initial idea.

I returned a week later to co-write with Beckah, and Shock played the track for me. It was bananas! As I listened there in their home studio, words immediately came flooding to my mind, but they were not the normal dancing or club ideas I had previously formulated. The words "Shake Heaven" were what came out, and as I sang the words, in a call and response type fashion, Beckah Shae began repeating after me.

Me: Gonna Shake Heaven! Her: Gonna Shake Heaven!

Me: Join in together! Her: Join in together!

Me: This is how we do it! Her: This is how...

"Stop!" I interrupted. I apologized and began searching for other words, ashamed that the phrase had actually come to my mind. Beckah Shae was quick to stop me. "No! That's perfect, Montell. You have got to say that." I argued that it would be corny and that some might think I was attempting to use the fame of the original song to exalt myself into becoming something great in whatever new place God was leading me. But I felt in my heart that this time, it wasn't about me. Was it possible that something as huge as "This Is How We Do It" could be used to bring God glory? After being nearly begged to leave that line in the song, the chorus would conclude with, "We're taking back the music!" The verses were written with my insecurity and uncertainty in mind regarding "What's it gonna look like? What's it gonna be like? What's it gonna sound like? I wanna know." But in faith, I declared that this was a mission He was leading and so I was willing to take the journey in hopes others would join in to make the name of Jesus higher than any other, especially my own. This song became more than an anthem, but my life theme song for the season we were about to enter into. We completed the song that day. I recall driving home playing the ruff mix from Shock in the car all the way home on repeat for nearly four hours. I don't recall hearing the voice of God audibly many times in my life, but at that moment, I can remember being overwhelmed with the feeling of Him saying to me, "You see? It can be done."

I had made gospel song offerings on albums here and there throughout my entire career. Those were created to support my albums and my projects and my fame. This song was created with no agenda or project in mind. God was simply showing me that if I will respond, He will too. The whole deal with faith is that it requires us to move or respond first. In all truth, He still calls us and draws us to Himself first before we ever take our first steps toward Him. Real talk, many of you reading or hearing these words right now also know you have been called to something greater and have delayed in responding. It's my prayer God is as patient with you as He was with me.

TWENTY-ONE

Giving It All Away

We have now arrived to the forward presented in the opening pages of this book. During a midweek service while Kristin and I were assisting the pastors, a message from our friend Johnson Bowie rocked our world and began a work in each of us simultaneously while we were each in two different places in the room. On the concrete floor of that Fusion young adult ministry at Victory World Church, we both heard from God that we needed to move from the norm into the unknown. It seemed that our God moments were accelerated now, and we no longer had the luxury of moving at our own pace. There were three very specific things I wrestled with on the floor that night, and with each concern, I received an answer.

1. *God, how will I provide for my family?* That was my first question. The answer? I was never the provider for my family. He was. I was just the vehicle God used to transport the provision He always made for us. If I could wrap my mind around the idea that He was the provider and not myself, I would experience a level of freedom beyond comprehension. My family would become the beneficiaries of His benefits rather than what I could minimally do in my own strength.

2. *What will I do after music?* That was my next question. The answer was that I would minister to people. Not to just any people and not to just church people but to *nations*. The promise imparted into me that night was that of all the things I thought I had seen and experienced during my career, He would blow my mind and exceed anything I had previously imagined. That was a pretty big promise, because I had a pretty big imagination to accompany the things I had already experienced.

I had traveled the world and performed on some of the largest stages in stadiums with more than 70K people in the USA and even 100K in Europe. I had been invited to private islands owned by a sheik in the UAE and dined with his royal family in their palace. African dignitaries in Nigeria had smaller replicas of their palace in Abuja rebuilt in efforts to host me and the late Don Cornelius in their home. I had dined with dictators in Cuba, danced on stage with James Brown, and sang with, recorded and interviewed music legends. I had seen much in my music career, so the idea that His promises would exceed what I had already experienced, in addition to what I could think or imagine? That definitely had me curious. My journey in and out of the music business was so that I could go back and reach those like myself who have heard His voice and not answered. God allowed me to see those places and do those things not for my own success but so that He could have access. My final inquiry would be the most difficult question to ask. This was where I wrestled with God like Jacob, for the words that would come next from my mouth would solidify my commitment to truly laying down my life as I had known it.

3. *God, will You take away my taste for the things of this world?* This was the most important question I had ever asked God. I knew that once things became challenging,

I could always go back to my old ways and my old hustle to provide for my family. I was willing to go anywhere and do anything to get what was needed to survive. I sang at a J.R. Crickets club in Atlanta one evening while drunken women shouted obscenities at me to "Stop all that talking and show your private parts!" in efforts just to secure $500. I degraded myself on countless occasions, and knew with my own strength, I was incapable of walking away from the addictive life I had lived in and was dying in. I had to know that I wouldn't go back; otherwise it would make no sense to attempt this walk of faith in the first place. God, if I'm going to fail You and shame You, don't allow me to start something I can't finish.

His answer was, "My grace is sufficient enough." That wasn't the answer I was seeking, but even today, my youngest son Skyler wisely speaks, "Dad, when we ask God for things, sometimes He says no." Yes, He could take the taste away; my longing for fame and fortune could be removed. And no, He could not promise that I would not make mistakes along the way or do things that would fall short of Christian expectations. But me, shaming God? We would have to think pretty highly of ourselves to think we were capable of doing that. He assured me that no matter what I did, He was secure in being God and would be fine, despite my failures.

Kristin and I both eventually picked ourselves up and walked away that evening knowing what we needed to do but not knowing exactly how to do it. We had marching orders with no destination of where to march.

I attended a men's spiritual retreat in October of 2010, and during that time away, the Lord really wrecked me (in a good way). I felt that in order for God to do His part, I would first have to do mine. I returned home following my three-day sabbatical and told Kristin to cancel every show and engagement we had remaining on our calendar. Any event that we would not get sued for canceling, I instructed her to remove it. There was no alternate source of income and no plan B. We would become completely reliant on Jesus to be our sustaining source upon doing this. We were shutting everything down completely.

Even as I was laying my life on the altar, parts of me didn't want to die. Pride on several occasions would rise up and say, "You can't leave! The music business needs you. The fans love you!" In efforts to verify if this was true, I began to announce that I was thinking of retiring from the music industry. There were no major or minor attempts from anyone or any part of the music business world to hinder my departure. I had a concert scheduled in Arizona around Halloween weekend in a venue that held 3,500 in a well-populated college town. The event was promoted well, yet only seven people showed up. Seven, one of which was my road manager. That night I performed my full show, with everything I had within me, for seven people. That very night, my taste for performance faded. I would find myself worshiping at church that same weekend where over four services and nearly 2000 people were in attendance each time. They were there with their hands lifted high—but not for me. Friday night, seven showed up for me. Saturday and Sunday, 10,000 showed up for Him. He was truly removing the taste and desire for fame away from me, but it wasn't painless.

I have always been aware that no man can open a door God shuts and vice versa. At this time, all doors were closed and there were no windows, trap doors, or secret escape hatches present. But then one opportunity presented itself. The senior pastor of Victory World

Church, Dennis Rouse, asked me to have breakfast with him. I had developed a relationship with the music director of the ministry at that time, and even though I was serving and volunteering regularly in the music ministry, I had never really entertained the idea of working for a church. What I didn't know at that time and didn't find out until several years later, was that the Lord had spoken to him and told him someone famous would be leaving the secular music world and would be the next worship pastor at Victory. I was completely unaware of this, and of course, he didn't share this with me at the time. I wasn't officially offered a job nor was I hired right there, but an invitation was presented that the position may be available if I were interested.

I left the meeting knowing there were no options remaining. Promoters were not beating down my door for shows, labels weren't seeking me out to sign any deals and publishers weren't trying to get my next penned hit for their artists. There's a difference in "falling off" and coming to a standstill, but to those on the outside looking in, they can't distinguish between the two. I still had a choice before me; God was just gracious enough to limit my potential for answering incorrectly. My entire life I had chosen other options that didn't put Him first. I was being positioned to receive the biggest blessing in my life, whether I wanted it or not.

I shared the opportunity with my wife, who handles our home finances. She was more aware of where our life and future existence currently stood and urged and encouraged me that we needed to consider the Lord was leading us to taking a position in the ministry. We prayerfully determined that if the church would have me, I would come on staff as a worship leader at the beginning of 2011. This would enable us to get our affairs in order for the greatest transition we would ever make.

Over the next few weeks, we sold our dream home that we built from the ground up for only a fraction of what it was worth. We had it on the market for over a year generating little or no interest, but upon my acceptance of the music position at the church, the house sold within 3 weeks. We sold our cars. Between accommodating the IRS and downsizing our lives to become more simplistic, sincere, and sacrificial to fit the new lifestyle of working at a church full-time, every move we made was drastic. What we didn't sell, we gave away. Kristin gave away her entire Rolodex of contacts and relationships to other booking agents who had been her competitors in the past. It was not only me who was leaving the business, but she was laying her life down as well. Beyond the material things, we laid our pride on the altar and allowed any evidence of fame to be sacrificed. I believed that my new start in the church would be the beginning of my life in obscurity. Nothing could have been further from the truth.

I was learning that a man and woman can have the whole world, and without Christ they are bankrupt and have nothing. One may also have nothing, but in Christ, be the wealthiest man and woman this side of heaven. This story is far from over, but I'll save that for the full autobiography. There is just one more chapter I'd like to share with you now.

TWENTY-TWO

Becoming Unfamous

I woke up January 1, 2011, and remember it as being the first time I had ever been truly free. I believe I experienced spiritual schizophrenia for so long that I lost my identity in the roles as husband, father, artist, songwriter, producer, businessman, sex symbol, and a bunch of other titles I don't care to name. The sights and smells of that morning are so vivid to me, even to this day. Of all the different Montells I had to be, that day I woke up as only one person. I was the Montell that God loved the most. I cannot describe the peace that came along with that realization, but I assure you it is a feeling that you can't pay for and you won't experience outside of Christ. He provides a peace that passes all understanding. Only He can do that. I am living that peace, even today.

I would also begin working at the church in January of 2011, only a few short days after my "one Montell" revelation. On my first day on the job, I knew the church had made a big mistake. As I entered my office, there was a signed and framed document on my desk stating that I was now a licensed pastor. Whoa. I immediately searched for a number to call human resources and inform them of their grave error.

I spent quite some time that day attempting to correct the people who had hired me. I believed I was brought on staff to be a worship leader; I would write songs and lead worship but I had no idea that I was now considered a pastor. They assured me that the ministry position I agreed to was indeed pastoral, and it was now a part of my title, along with the ability to marry, bury and dip (baptize). I was shocked. I called my wife to explain to her how the ministry must have been out of their minds to hire a former R&B star to be a pastor. I understood how to lead people...but *pastor* them? My new title would become the object of ridicule around our home for a few weeks, as my kids would say to their friends, "Yeah, my dad is clergy now." My wife even jumped in on the fun until one day a friend reminded her that this also now made her the pastor's wife. *The first lady.* She declares she threw up in her mouth a little at that revelation. Honestly, our history with men and women who held those esteemed titles in ministry caused us to shy away from accepting the responsibility that came with the title. It would take months before I walked in the purpose of loving people the way God desired me to in my new role as a pastor.

With the new position also came the old temptation. The enemy has no new tricks, only really good old ones. Just prior to our retirement from the music business, there were no offers for concerts, shows, or recording deals on the table. Following our acceptance of the ministry calling, we were offered nearly one million dollars in show money, automobiles, tour opportunities, and endorsements during the year of 2011 alone. How could anyone in their right mind turn down opportunities like that? Why would they? We were out of our mind, but thankfully we were on His. It would take His strength and promises to sustain us as the offers continuously came in. We would often laugh to keep from crying at the amounts and frequency the enemy was seeking to woo us back to him following our full sold-out commitment to Christ. The Devil must have been pretty upset, because he offered us pie in the sky and threw in the very expensive kitchen sink to boot.

The first song I ever sang on the Victory platform was "Moving Forward" by Ricardo Sanchez and Israel Houghton. It was not only my theme song and a spiritual movement for the church in that season, but it would become my heart's desire and the soundtrack to our lives:

I'm not going back

I'm moving ahead

I'm here to declare to you

My past is over

In you, all things are made new

Surrendered my life to Christ

I'm moving, moving forward

The Lord had truly taken away our desires for the world and replaced them with the desires for His heart, but that did not stop the attempts from the enemy to make sure we were secured in our choice of faith over fame. One of the things I did to guard myself against the constant call to return to my old life was determine that I would never sing "This Is How We Do It" or any of my R&B material ever again. I realized the song had become an idol to me; I could worship it and look for it to be my provider over God Himself. I could accept one engagement, fly first class with four star hotel accommodations, and sing a four-minute song to earn my son's or daughter's school tuition for a semester in just one day. That option was no longer on the table, so saying "the Lord will provide" became our reality. And He never disappointed. We watched Him perform miracle after miracle that we didn't expect or anticipate. Today, I am able to sing the song again. I realize that I determined I would never sing that song again, yet God never said that. He is now using my classic hip-hop music to reach millions for ministry. This is the journey from how we do it to how *He* do it.

As I now began functioning in my pastoral role, people from both inside and outside of the church still recognized me from my prior R&B life and paid respects for my musical accomplishments. I often found myself purposely diminishing myself so that no resemblance or residue of pride would remain. It seemed like the more I attempted to humble myself, more opportunities presented themselves for me to be exalted. I became so paranoid at consciously attempting to remain humble; I feared appearing too humble would be viewed as false humility. I didn't want to disappoint the ministry leaders around me, or the Christians who were now watching my transition to see if it was authentic or godly enough, and myself by failing to accomplish reaching the huge destiny God placed before me. I would spend the next four years in ministry attempting to become unfamous so that the name of Jesus would become *more famous* through me.

I once heard a saying that becoming selfless isn't thinking less of your self but thinking of yourself less. At every turn, I made attempts to declare that my name, notoriety, and fame didn't mean anything to me. I drove a 1999 black Honda Accord for four years in efforts to remain true to the humbling process I endured for a season. I didn't like it, and by no means am I saying it was my choice; but in efforts to become debt free and lose the borrowed lifestyle mentality to survive in the new world of ministry, the Lord had me in a season of showing me my worth was not determined in what I was driving or what I was wearing. I would pull up to stop lights and be ashamed of being recognized in a vehicle that I felt didn't speak prominence. God was still breaking pride off me. Back in the day, the vision boards Kristin and I used to create would have our dream house, Bentley cars, yachts, and name brand material possessions high above any of the desires His heart had for us. In reality, I don't believe we ever had anything regarding faith posted on those boards. I was experiencing that my name, by itself, had no real lasting value outside of Christ. But inside of Christ is a whole different story.

There are only two Scriptures I will share in this entire book, and the first is found in the very first book of the bible.

I'll make you a great nation and bless you. I'll make you famous; you'll be a blessing. Genesis 12:2-3 (MSG)[3]

God desires to make us famous. He desires to bless us so that we may be a blessing so that nations and even generations can be blessed through us. I submit to you that there is a distinct difference in God making us famous and our making ourselves famous. I know this because I lived it. People will continuously rise in stardom and eventually fall. Some may sustain the spotlight and burn longer than others, but ultimately, we will find no matter what area of life where success is attainable, only those who glorify God have any potential of sustaining fame.

We were not designed to carry fame. *He* desires to make your name great. When we make efforts to achieve this feat on our own, we are, in essence, attempting to be God. I know this to be true as well, as I lived it.

"This Is How We Do It" is something far greater than a big song from the 90s. The fact that He would orchestrate the success of a song and the rise and fall of a man only to rise again to tell of His restoring power to resurrect what was once dead back to life is an expression of God's love for mankind and husbands and wives. God raised Jesus Christ from the dead back then, and He is still bringing the dead back to life today. Careers, marriages, families, and dreams are still being lifted from the grave daily; we only need look for it in our friends, neighbors, coworkers, and even our own lives to see miracles happening every day.

Our marriage ministry book will hopefully be a physical representation of God's love made tangibly accessible to enrich the lives of millions of marriages in this and the coming generations. Many reading or listening to this right now are experiencing something dead or dormant receive life, just from the faithful words expressed in hope through Jesus Christ.

In the entertainment industry, I thought I would die without music. I was in love with something that could never love me back. As I now reflect on my life in ministry as a pastor, I understand that music didn't make me; I made music. If life-giving musicians, producers, and songwriters are not creating material that in some way honors the gift of music that God has given us, we will see a steady decline in the content and creativity in music. The gift is God's; the gimmicks are ours. Reliance on reinventing ourselves to stay relevant is a symptom that the gift given to us is being rented out and depleted for our own achievements rather than developed and enhanced prior to returning the property back to the original owner. Another book called *The Power of Music* is also in the works, and an excerpt of this message is available to view at www.victoryatl.com under archived messages.[4]

As I complete these words, the future is uncertain regarding our next steps in ministry. I may travel the world speaking and counseling alongside my wife on how God is a healer of covenant relationships between men and women as we watch Him miraculously transform a million marriages (or more) through the power of Jesus. I may possibly even re-enter the entertainment world to offer hope to those who were lost like me. The promise to reach nations is no small task. The Jordan family may unite to show viewing audiences what a modern Christ-following family looks like. We may share how we strive to live godly in a society that is becoming more godless and try not to look crazy. Perhaps the very act of attempting this is crazy. I may look for opportunities to share what fatherhood looks like to a generation of youth who have lost their identity.

This is what I am called to do. This is what Kristin and I are called to do together. I may pastor a church someday, if that is what God desires. I may continue as a worship pastor leading people into the presence of God. I may do all of these things, some of these things, or none of them at all. I will do whatever God leads us into. What He takes us to, He will most definitely take us through. This has been the journey from how we do it to how He do it. Bad grammar and all, it's not any less true.

If no one ever remembers my name, they will remember the name I called on: *Jesus*. Now here is the second and final Scripture presented in this book, as promised.

"If you decide that it's a bad thing to worship God, then choose a god you'd rather serve—and do it today. Choose one of the gods your ancestors worshiped from the country beyond The River, or one of the gods of the Amorites, on whose land you're now living. As for me and my family, we'll worship God." Joshua 24:15 (MSG)[5]

PS. We are hoping our lives become a blessing to all people, especially those husbands and wives in need of hope for their marriages. We are here for you. Your next steps are at www.montellandkristin.com.

PSS. More specifically, if any entertainers and athletes are reading or hearing this and you desire to speak directly with Kristin and me, we want to make ourselves available to you. The business didn't equip us with resources or anyone who could help us navigate the waters of marriage and fame. Perhaps your story will one day become the testimony to assist the journey another couple needs to survive.

ENDNOTES

[1] American Psychological Association (APA): Famous. (n.d.). Dictionary.com Unabridged. Retrieved July 10, 2015, from Dictionary.com website: http://dictionary.reference.com/browse/famous

[2] *You Are So Beautiful* by Joe Cocker, 1974, written by B. Carleton/B. Preston

[3] Genesis 12:2-3 *The Message (MSG) copyright © 1993, 1994, 1995, 1996, 2000, 2001, 2002 by Eugene H. Peterson*

[4] The Power of Music www.victoryatl.com April 15, 2012 (sermon archives)

[5] Joshua 24:15 *The Message (MSG) Copyright © 1993, 1994, 1995, 1996, 2000, 2001, 2002 by Eugene H. Peterson*

Leave your testimony at:
www.montellandkristin.com

Reach us directly at:
Montell@montellandkristin.com
Kristin@montellandkristin.com
booking@montellandkristin.com